Praise for
Where's There Smoke, There's Dinner

"I laughed, gasped, wept—sometimes all in the same paragraph—when reading *Where There's Smoke, There's Dinner: Stories of a Seared Childhood* by Regi Carpenter. Growing up as the youngest of the exuberant, notorious, and often destitute "Carpenter kids" of Clayton, NY, Regi is resourceful against all the odds. This is a candid story of desperate measures, explosive humor, and, ultimately, the sanity behind seeming madness. It teaches a new understanding of family love. Brilliant writing!"

—*Jo Radner, reviewer for the National Storytelling Network's magazine*

"Giver of story, giver of light: Regi Carpenter takes lived experience and imagined choices and shapes them into what listeners—and now readers—need in their deepest hunger. To hear her tell is to live a way of seeing existence—becoming existence—in a world where it's okay to ask questions about why we exist at all. To be in her presence is to know golden genius. And now this book can carry her spirit into minds and hearts allowing her in: welcome, readers seeking treasure, to this trove of tales that glow."

—*Katharyn Howd Machan, author of* Redwing: Voices from 1888 *and* Wild Grapes: Poems of Fox

"I am a believer that the Lord works in wondrous ways and especially through the stories of Regi Carpenter in *Where There's Smoke, There's Dinner: Stories of a Seared Childhood* as I laughed and cried with the brilliant writer Carpenter! Do yourself a favor and go get *Where There's Smoke, There's Dinner* at once! You'll be in for a literary treat if you do!"

—*Nancy Slonim Aronie, founder of The Chilmark Writing Workshop and former Harvard University professor*

"Regi Carpenter's stories celebrate the glorious and gut wrenching life of the youngest Carpenter clan growing up on a small town on a big river with an undercurrent."

—*Loren Niemi, Produce of Two Chairs Telling, Minneapoils, Minnesota*

Where There's Smoke,

There's Dinner

Published by Familius LLC, www.familius.com

Familius books are available at special discounts for bulk purchases, whether for sales promotions or for family or corporate use. For more information, contact Familius Sales at 559-876-2170 or email orders@familius.com.

Library of Congress Cataloging-in-Publication Data
2016947414

Print ISBN 9781942934400
Ebook ISBN 9781944822231
Hardcover ISBN 9781944822248

Printed in the United States of America

Edited by Kelsey Cummings
Cover design by David Miles
Book design by Maggie Wickes

10 9 8 7 6 5 4 3 2 1

First Edition

Where There's Smoke, There's Dinner

STORIES

OF A

SEARED

CHILDHOOD

REGI CARPENTER

For Tim, the pinball wizard,

and

Will and Sam—now you know where you come from.

Contents

Introduction: The Lucky Caul

Regina Coeli, O Queen of Heaven, rejoice: alleluia;
For the child whom you so nobly bore: alleluia;
Rose from the dead, as he foretold: alleluia;
Pray for us now, we ask of you: alleluia.

I am the fifth and last child of Carl Henry Carpenter and Josephine Agnes Kneip—the tail end of a succession that begins with David Richard, Timothy John, Cynthia Jean, and Mary Agnes. On the day of my birth, August 15—the day Catholics assume Mary, Queen of the Heavens, rose to live at the right hand of the Father and her Holy Son, Jesus—my parents name me Regina Marie, which means "Queen Mary." *Alleluia.*

It starts when we're living the low life in Lebanon, Pennsylvania. My father is traveling door to door trying to sell life insurance while my mother is in our run-down three-bedroom apartment that's too close to the tracks. She's in the hallway when the childbirth pains come upon her. As she reaches down with a curious hand, her fingers come up wet, sticky, and the color of a cardinal.

"I could feel the umbilical cord protruding between my legs. I had had four children, so I knew that wasn't right. I stood up all the way in the taxi."

"Why didn't Dad come with you?"

Her look tells me I have a horn growing out of my head.

"Well, who would have stayed with the children?"

I am a dead baby wearing a caul. A caul is a sheath of skin so thin it's like a veil, or a shroud, or a parchment with a promise written on it from one world to another. Mine says *Happy Birthday, Thursday's child. You have far to go.*

A caul is a talisman sought after to prevent drowning.

I breathe air instead of water, and they whisk me away to an incubator. My mother goes to a hospital bed in a room she shares with another fallen virgin with a lazy bladder who flips the light switch in the middle of the night and sees my mother bleeding out in the hospital bed for a baby she barely knows. She is resurrected on blood transfusions but too weak to go home for months. It's a miracle. *Alleluia.*

Now my father has the poor working man's dilemma. With no wife at home, should he work or take care of the kids? Work—keep apartment, no one to take care of the kids. Not work—lose apartment, take care of the kids. What to do? Work.

"Reg, I called everybody up to come help us, but no one could come. I even called Edna."

"Do you mean crazy squirrel lady Edna?"

"She was my last choice."

Dave, Tim, Cindi (did we ever call her Cynthia?), and Mary go into temporary but separate foster care. My father drops them off one by one in the gray Buick. The tires squeal as he tears out of the driveways.

My mother lays alone for three days in the hospital bed.

"'Where is my baby, nurse? Is it a boy or a girl? Is the baby alright?' This was the 1950s, Regi. The nurses wouldn't tell me a thing. They thought it would be easier that way. They were trying to be nice."

She lays there alone for three days wondering, "Do I have a child?" I lay there alone for three days wondering, "Do I have a mother?" Those two questions would be spirited between my mother and me for over forty years.

Regina Coeli, O Queen of Heaven, rejoice: alleluia;
For the child whom you so nobly bore: alleluia;
Rose from the dead, as he foretold: alleluia;
Pray for us now, we ask of you: alleluia.

How I Became a Carpenter

I grew up in Clayton, a small town in northern New York where Lake Ontario and the St. Lawrence River open their mouths to give each other a big, wet kiss. Carpenters have been living in Clayton for five generations. In the 1600s, when our name was "Charpentier," we fled Quebec and murderous Canadian Protestantism with other French-speaking Roman Catholic fugitives. Arriving at the rapids of the St. Lawrence River, we climbed into a flimsy boat, said a Hail Mary, and rode until we landed at a place that was mild and manageable: Clayton. Along the open-channel side of town, Catholics established themselves as boat builders, guides, trappers, blacksmiths, lumberjacks, and fishermen. Large families lived in one-room shacks on the river's edge. We mined the rock quarries on the thousand and more islands and built the majestic St. Mary's Church and, behind it, a shrine to the Blessed Virgin Mary.

I was wandering around Clayton one recent day when I found myself on Union Street staring at the empty plot where my Grandma Carpenter's house stood before a fire burned it down. The foundation was still there, and her hollyhocks were in bloom. I remembered my mother flicking her eyelashes on my cheek as we lay in the grassy mound at the corner of Union and Theresa Streets. "Butterfly kisses," she called them. I laughed when I got to the top of the hill on Alexandria Street where my brothers Tim and Dave taught Cindi how to ride a bike by pushing her down the hill and straight into the St. Lawrence River. Finally, I meandered over to Strawberry Lane to check on the horseradish patch Dad and Uncle Rip planted over fifty years ago. As I strolled through the uneven streets of Clayton, I swear every blade of grass was calling my name.

Why do I feel so at home here? Is it because I grew up in Clayton? What makes someone feel like they belong somewhere, anyway? I questioned.

Then I noticed the fabulous shoes in the window of the new tourist shop, and I had to have them. Next to the pretty pumps was a bumper sticker that answered all my deep and soulful musings:

A scar is a tattoo with a better story.

Exactly.

Each of my brothers and sisters had scars under their chins by the time they were six years old. Cindi's and Mary's chins kissed the curb on the corner of James Street and Mary Street while they were roller skating. Dave said a tree jumped in front of his bike. Tim mysteriously got his during religious education. (Holy Week was never the same for Tim.) After each injury, my siblings stumbled home, bloodied and babbling, and showed the gash to our pop.

"Are you going to take me to the doctor, Dad?"

"You don't need to go to the doctor. You just need a butterfly bandage. You'll be perfectly fine."

Dad had a cure for everything. If it was viral or bacterial, the cure involved onions. To cure a cold, we ate raw onions. For a cough, we wore mustard plasters covered with raw diced onions on our chests. The fever treatment was thin slices of onion warmed in an iron skillet, pressed against the soles of our feet, and held there overnight by wool socks. Crazy, but they worked.

If, however, we had a sore, a cut, a gash, or a gaping wound, he applied a butterfly bandage, a technique he had perfected during World War II. Take a large adhesive bandage, cut it in the shape of butterfly wings, put one sticky piece on one side of the gash and the other on the opposite, and bring the flesh together for makeshift stitches. Voilà: the butterfly bandage!

My mother was absolutely powerless against the butterfly bandage. "Carl! These children need medical attention!"

"Josephine, there I was in the Second World War on the island of Luzon in the Philippines. The war was raging all around me. Picture bombs dropping, grenades being launched, flames and smoke everywhere. Then a good buddy of mine steps on a landmine and blows his leg off. He takes some shrapnel in his lungs, and then he gets a bullet in the middle of his brain. Did we take him to the doctor? We did not. We applied the butterfly bandage, and he was perfectly fine. If it's good enough for a World War II veteran, it's good enough for a Carpenter kid."

"Oh, for God's sake," she sighed, rolling her eyes and resigning to her fate.

By the time I was six, I had no scar, no butterfly bandage, and no makeshift stitches like my brothers and sisters. They kindly interpreted this for me:

"You know what that means, don't ya?"

"What?"

"You're probably not a Carpenter."

"Really?"

The sibling circle of menace tightened.

"Yeah, you're probably not even Catholic!"

Holy smokes! Not Catholic? Not a Carpenter? What?

"You take it back, take it back!" I yelled and raised my noogie fingers to show them I really was talking business. Secretly, though, I was worried.

"Mommy, how many kids did you have?"

"That I know of, sweetheart?"

That troubled me. I didn't pursue it. Instead, I appealed for some divine intervention:

"In the name of the Father, the Son, and the Holy Spirit, dear Saint Aldegundis, patron saint of gashes and wounds, I pray for a reverse blessing. Do not heal me of a gash or wound; rather, inflict one upon me underneath my chin so I know I am a Carpenter. Please don't make it too disfiguring. In Jesus's sweet name I pray. Amen."

And one hot, sweaty, sultry summer night, St. Aldegundis answered my prayer.

―――――――――

We're living on Riverside Drive across from the Mercier's Beach dock. My father is away most of the summer being a traveling salesman—emphasis on *traveling*.

"Try and hold down the fort, Josephine," he instructs her as he prepares to leave.

"Roger that, Big Buddy. Wilko and out," she replies, saluting him with two fingers at her eyebrows.

Mary and I are playing in the dining room. Mary is ten, and I'm six. She is my best friend. We play the same game every night: cops and robbers. Mary is always the cop, and I am always the robber. I always get caught. I'm always guilty. I'm always tortured. I'm the youngest of five—I know my role. Standing still, I wait while Mary sneaks up behind me, wraps her arms around my waist, and throws me onto the dining room chair.

"You have been found guilty by a jury of your peers and are sentenced to DEATH. Wait here while I go and get the rope," she spits while pointing a finger in my face.

"Okay."

She disappears into the kitchen and comes back with Mom's best dish towels. Quickly binding my wrists and legs together, she then stuffs a dirty sock into my mouth.

"Now go to the electric chair," she commands and points to the green couch in the living room.

I stand and start doing the electrocution hop. About six inches from the couch, a beam of ethereal light breaks through the ceiling and illuminates the green couch. I hear the sounds of a heavenly harp. An angelic hand reaches down, grabs my ankle, and tugs. I lurch forward. My chin hits the sharp edge of the couch and splits open. Blood spurts. Mary screams.

"MOM! Regi needs you! I didn't do it!" She runs away. *She runs away.*

My mother comes in, sees me, sighs, and rolls her eyes.

"Oh, for God's sake," she whispers, untying me and taking the sock out of my mouth.

"Are you going to apply the butterfly bandage, Mommy?" I blubber.

The corners of her mouth turn up, and she gets a little twinkle in her eye. "Oh, no, honey. Only Daddy can apply the butterfly bandage properly. I'm afraid I am going to have to take you to the doctor's," she purrs and skips into the kitchen to make the call.

"Take you to the doctor's" sounds like an echo in the mountains. It reverberates throughout the entire house. My brothers and sisters scramble down the stairs and encircle me.

"You're going to the doctor's, you spoiled brat!" they snarl.

"I know I am but what are *you*?"

Mom comes out of the kitchen and hands me a dry blue washcloth to put under my chin. "Let's go," she says as she walks out the front door.

My siblings form a birth-order gauntlet by the door: Dave, Tim, Cindi, and then Mary. As I sashay by them, they hiss, "We. Hate. You."

"I'm goin' to the doctor's," I sing tauntingly and stick out my tongue.

My mother is waiting for me on the porch. It's such a hot, humid night that the air is fuzzy and vacuum-packs around our bodies. The sun is setting on the St. Lawrence River, so both sky and water are tangerine-orange colored. It's Friday night on the Catholic side of town, so the smell of fish fry hangs in the air and mingles with the scents of stinky seaweed, fetid fish, and that soft briny cheese northern New Yorkers love to eat on Saltine crackers with French's mustard. Limburger cheese has an aroma best described as "carcass."

Mom and I walk down the porch steps and turn right onto Riverside Drive. She walks a few paces ahead of me. Her hips sway to the rhythm of the waves beating against Mercier's dock. She is wearing a plaid pleated skirt and a turtleneck with no sleeves. That turtleneck tells you everything you need to know about my mother. The neck says cold, but the arms confirm hot. Her guitar-shaped body is moving to the rhythm of a Latin song only she can hear: *Bah da dee, bah dah dah dee. Bah da dee, bah dah dah dee, bah da dee da dee da, bah dah deee daaah.*

The eyes in the back of her head are watching me. The invisible line that connects a mother and her child is taut. We meander up Riverside Drive, make a right at the 1812 war cannons, turn onto John Street, go past the library, and hang another right on Hugunin Street. Dr. Heady, the new doctor in town, is waiting for us on the stoop. He's tall and skinny. His slicked-back black hair is shiny and stiff, and his five o'clock stubble is working overtime. He's chain-smoking. When we are near enough, he removes the washcloth from under my chin and sucks in air between his teeth.

"Ooh, Josephine. She's going to need stitches and a shot of No-vocain. It'll affect her mouth. She might not be able to talk a while."

"Could you give her two shots, doctor?"

"Doctors do no harm, Josephine. We do no harm," he reminds her.

In the office, he plops me on top of a wooden block in the red chair, then turns on a light so bright it makes my retinas bubble. I watch his long, scarecrow-skinny fingers take the silver needle and black thread down, through, and up, down, through, and up, seven times. *Snip, snip.* When it's over, he hands me a lollipop, which I plan on eating very slowly in front of my brothers and sisters. It's dark when my mother and I walk down his steps.

"Let's take the long way home," Mom decides. We hang a right on John Street and walk toward the Catholic playground, where no one is allowed to have any fun, and stroll over to the shrine, where the Blessed Virgin Mary lives. The shrine to the Blessed Virgin Mary in Clayton, New York, is the most beautiful place on earth. It's made of white limestone taken from Quarry Island. It glows day and night. The shrine is made in the shape of a candle flame. There are wide, thick, curving steps at the front of the shrine. (All us Catholic kids get pictures taken here on the day of our First Communion.) Flanking the steps are two tiered rows of red votive candles. The statue of the Virgin Mary levitates on a small ledge at the back of the shrine. A fountain flows from her feet and collects in a pool at the back. After church, us Catholic kids pitch pennies into the pool and make wishes. The Virgin's arms are outstretched in a gesture of universal compassion. Above her is the very first mystery novel I ever read:

I am the Immaculate Conception.

It's an unsolvable mystery.

My mother and I sit down on the benches. As I kick my legs back and forth, she looks off into a distance I'll never see. Finally, she turns back, runs her hand through my curly hair, and squeezes my neck.

"Pretty big day for you, huh, sport?" she asks.

"Uh-huh," I mumble. My tongue hangs out of my mouth like a dog's.

"Would you like to light a votive candle?"

"Uhhh-huh," I say, and my eyes sparkle. She gives me fifty cents, and I add my little light to the others. My mother and I sit on the benches for the longest time just listening to the sounds of the St. Lawrence River, the night birds, the crickets, and all the songs singing inside of our heads.

After the longest time, she turns to me and says, "Well, whaddya say we head on home, sport? Where we belong?" She stands and smooths her skirt. Her hand reaches out for mine. We leave the shrine and walk hand in hand down Riverside Drive—where Carpenters and Charpentiers have walked now for hundreds of years, ever since they got into a boat with people like themselves and went searching for a place to call home.

Peanut Butter and Jelly

"Run, Dick, run. See Dick run. Run, Jane, run. See Jane run." That's what my classmates drone while I stare at the brightly colored murals on every wall of my second grade classroom. One summer, Professor DiStefano, Clayton Central School's art teacher, turned Mrs. Kittle's second grade classroom into the Sistine Chapel for kids. He painted monkeys swinging from palm trees on the hot water pipes. Jack climbs the beanstalk up to the loudspeaker. Fairies flitter by the light switch. Rapunzel's long golden braid hangs from ceiling to floor at the back picture window, while Sleeping Beauty sings to a bluebird by the moon-shaped clock. All day long, I listen to the walls talk.

Fee, fi, fo, fum, someone still sucks her thumb! chastises the Giant.

"See Jane run."

"She can't read? Her IQ test proves she has a superior intellect. Why can't she read?" my mother interrogates Mrs. Kittle, my bewildered teacher. I didn't *want* to read about Jane running when I could listen to the walls.

Fee, fi, fo, fum, everyone thinks you're dumb!

"She can't read!" my mother cries.

After deeming me deficient, Mrs. Kittle sends me to remedial reading with Mrs. Thompson. Her walls are white except for the large alphabet cards displayed throughout the room.

On our first day together, she holds an alphabet card close to my face. "What sound does this letter make?" Mrs. Thompson asks.

"I don't know," I answer honestly.

"This letter speaks like a motorboat," she instructs, then demonstrates: "buhbuhbuhbuhbuhbuhbuhbuhbuh." Her cheeks flap like sails in the wind.

"Buhbuhbuhbuhbuhbuhbuhbuhbuh," I repeat and imagine a double-decker tour boat pulling away from the Clayton town dock. The boat is just like the one my father pilots for the scenic tours of the 1000 Islands Boat Line.

"What does this letter say?" asks Mrs. Thompson hopefully as she displays another card.

"I don't know," is my forthright response as I gaze out the window.

"This letter is like an old grandfather who's hard of hearing." She cups her ear and pretends she can't hear and then says "eh? But sometimes"—she elongates the word "sometimes" so it sounds like *sssummmmtimessss*—"it eats too much," and here Mrs. Thompson pushes her belly way out and grabs it with her hands and says "aaaah." Then she wipes her face with her sleeve.

"Aaaah," I repeat and grab my belly like I'm about to pop.

"How about this letter?" Mrs. Thompson asks.

"Um." I pretend I'm thinking.

"This letter sounds like a tea kettle boiling over. T-t-t-t-t-t-t-t-t-t-t." Mrs. Thompson shakes her hips and arms like she's playing the maracas.

"T-t-t-t-t-t-t-t-t-t-t," I boil over.

"Now put those three sounds together," she says and holds the letters next to one another.

"Buhbuh aaaah t-t-t-t-t-t," I say and see a boat filled with big-bellied people drinking tea.

"A little faster now," she encourages me.

"Buh aaaah t-t."

"A little faster. Run the sounds together," she coaxes.

"Buh aaaah t-t," I sing. My eyebrows lift, and I extend my arms. "Buh aaaah t-t. Baat. Buh-at." I stare at the letters. The letters join together, and the sounds blend in my brain. It's a miracle.

"Mrs. Thompson!" I yell. "B-A-T spells *bat*! B-A-T spells *bat*!"

We chant and flap around the room. Mrs. Thompson teaches me to read. She gives me fairy tales and says they're our little secret. "Now that you can read, Regi, you have to learn how to write. Writers write what they know. What do you know, Regi?" Mrs. Thompson wonders.

———

We get our box of welfare food every two weeks at the back door of St. Mary's Catholic Convent alongside the other impoverished papists. We're on welfare because my father is usually in the veteran's hospital in Syracuse, New York. There's no disability pay yet. My mother works all summer long as a waitress at McCormick's Restaurant on the town dock. Tips are good, but after Labor Day, when tourist season is over, our pockets are turned out. We use the oven for heat and welfare food to feed our family of seven. The box always contains the same things: dry milk, dried eggs, flour, sugar, oil, lard, and Spam. There is also cat food–quality tuna fish, gelatinous canned corn beef, canned chopped ham, margarine, salt, a block of Day-Glo-colored soft cheese, and peanut butter. This peanut butter isn't Jif or Skippy. It's not a low-fat, low-salt, no-salt, creamy, crunchy, or non-hydrogenated peanut butter either. It is most definitely *not* an organic nut butter. It *is* a ten-pound can with black block lettering on a white label, property of the United States government, approved by the United States Department of Agriculture, not for individual resale PEANUT BUTTER.

"It's left over from World War I!" Mom says when she opens it. No amount of stirring can mix the oil floating on the top back into the nutty paste on the bottom. The peanut butter is so dry we practically have to jackhammer it out. Mom, no stranger to hardship, however, knows what to do.

Dough fried in peanut oil greets us in the morning. We have peanut butter and jelly sandwiches for lunch, peanut butter stew with potatoes and carrots discarded from the market for dinner, and peanut butter cookies for dessert. Sometimes she rolls the dry peanut butter, sugar, and margarine into balls and calls them "peanut butter bombs." Our standby, though, is peanut butter and jelly sandwiches—Wonder Bread slathered with peanut butter and topped with gooey grape jelly. When the bread and jelly run out, we pass the can from person to person. My brothers and mother dip two fingers into the peanut butter, my sisters and I use just one, and my father three, when he is home.

Writers write what they know. What do you know, Regi?

After school one afternoon, I sit with a blank sheet of white paper on the top porch step of my house. In my hand is a pencil so sharp it could take out the Cyclops's eye. I write my full name across the top and then write the title of my first play, a creation tale.

"How Peanut Butter and Jelly Sandwiches Came to Be"

by Regina Marie Carpenter

The characters:

Peanut Butter	Bread
Jelly	

"Hi, Jelly," says Peanut Butter, spread on Bread.

"Hi, Peanut Butter," says Jelly, also spread on Bread.

"How are you?" asks Peanut Butter.

"Fine," answers Jelly.

"That is good," says Peanut Butter.

"How are you?" asks Jelly.

"I am fine," says Peanut Butter.

"That is good," says Jelly.

"Yes," agrees Peanut Butter.

"Hey, would you like to get together sometime?" Peanut Butter asks.

"Yes. How about now?" asks Jelly.

"Okay!" answers Peanut Butter.

Peanut Butter and Jelly hug and later get married. That is how the first peanut butter and jelly sandwich was made. They lived happily ever after.

The End.

Self-Defense

It is April vacation in seventh grade when I have an epiphany. In a vision, there is a flash of lightning followed by the smell of sulfur, and my entire life rolls out before me in crystal clarity. I instantly know I am going to grow up to be a great artist living in abject poverty in the slums of New York City. Since New York City is a pretty dangerous place, it is obvious that in order to fulfill my destiny, I have to learn the art of self-defense.

After putting on my socks, boots, scarf, hat, coat, and mittens, I head out the front door of Carpenter's Grocery, my family's grocery store. I walk past the Catholic church, the Catholic convent, and the Catholic playground, where the swing set is in the shape of a cross. Walking up John Street, I stop at Hawn Memorial Library, a one-story brick building built in 1954 by Mr. John Hawn for the edification of the citizens of Clayton. Marching up the sloping sidewalk, I open the outer storm door, the middle storm door, and finally the inner storm door to approach the front desk where Mrs. Minnick, our town librarian, sits. Mrs. Minnick is the only town librarian we have ever had, and she is extraordinary in several ways.

First, she is shaped like a beefsteak tomato. Her salt-and-pepper hair sticks up off her head like the bristles of a brush. She has plush-carpet, square eyebrows and runny yolk eyes magnified ten to fifteen times behind thick Coke-bottle glasses. A soft, downy mustache graces her full, purplish lips. Not just remarkable to look at, Mrs. Minnick is also an incredible librarian—she knows where everything is in Hawn Memorial Library.

"Mrs. Minnick!" I begin excitedly. "There was a flash of lightning and a smell of sulfur, and I saw my life flash before me. I am going to be a great artist someday and live in abject poverty in the slums of New York City. New York City is so dangerous that I need to learn the art of self-defense in order to fulfill my destiny. Do you have any books on the art of self-defense, Mrs. Minnick?"

Her eyes shine like lard sizzling in a hot griddle, and she holds up a finger shaped like a kielbasa sausage.

"Regina, I have just the thing!" she exclaims and disappears into the back room. I wait dutifully and remember the good advice my father gave me.

"No good Catholic girl would be caught dead in the back room of the library," he warned me. "There's historical fiction and romance novels back there! Only Protestant girls would go into that back room. Don't risk damnation for a paperback," he sneered and puffed on his cigarette.

Ten minutes later, I hear stacks of books falling over. Mrs. Minnick emerges from behind the blue curtain with a small paperback in her hand.

"Regina, this is the book you need to fulfill your destiny!" she proclaims and slaps the book down on the front desk. I pick it up and read the title: *The Royal Canadian Air Force Book of Self-Defense*. Thank you, Canada!

After riffling through the card catalog to see what my neighbors are reading, I sign my name to the lending card and put it in place. Thanking Mrs. Minnick, I exit out the storm doors, turn right onto

John Street, walk past the Catholic playground, convent, and church, enter the front door of Carpenter's Grocery, and make a beeline for the living room. For the next week, I strategically turn my body into a killing machine.

Wearing a blue-striped polyester/cotton-blend gym uniform, I start Operation Self-Defense. Squat thrusts are followed by a bowl of chocolate ice cream. "Motivation is key to achieving a goal," the book says. Squats are followed by leg lunges and another big bowl of chocolate ice cream because *motivation is key to achieving a goal*. Push-ups, pull-ups, bicep curls, tricep curls, and abdominal crunches are done with machinelike precision and verve. After each vigorous exercise session, I reward myself with a big bowl of chocolate ice cream because *motivation is key to achieving a goal*. I gain ten pounds of muscle in one week. Once my body is in tip-top condition, I begin practicing my moves of self-defense. I do this by projecting myself into an imaginary scenario:

> My lithe, svelte body, robed in velvets and chiffons, floats through Central Park. An ostrich feather decorates my chapeau. Occasionally, I stop to wave to an adoring fan or sign an autograph for a young, impressionable child. Then my bat-like sonar hearing picks up the pitter-patter of a petty thief coming closer and closer to do something not at all nice. The attacker approaches from behind and reaches out for me. Unsuspectingly, I twirl, lift my leg, and jam my stiletto heels into his kneecap. He lunges forward. I thrust my elbow into his solar plexus. "Oof!" he cries. My palm shoves his nose cartilage up into his brain. He falls to the ground, writhing in agony and crying out, "Mercy, mercy!" I stand over him, drop to my knees, bring my lips to his ear, cry out like a banshee, and burst his eardrum! Then I stand and wave to my adoring fans and sign autographs for impressionable children.

My favorite move of self-defense is the carotid artery karate chop. The carotid artery takes all the blood to the brain, and if you hit it hard enough, you can knock someone flat in seconds. I pretend the white line on my brother Tim's football is someone's carotid artery. "Hi-yah, hi-yah, hi-yah, hi-yah, hi-yahhhhhh!" I scream as my hand slices through the air and crushes the white line.

By Friday, I feel ready to practice on a human being. Dad seems like the best candidate. He comes through the front door of Carpenter's Grocery every evening at 5:30, walks into the living room, lights a new cigarette from the butt of the one he's smoking, and sets down his briefcase full of chewing gum and playing cards.

"Dad!" I shout as I rush over to him. "There was a weird flash of lightning followed by a smell of sulfur, and I saw my life roll out before me. I am going to be a great artist someday and live in abject poverty in the slums of New York City. New York City is a pretty dangerous place, Dad, so in order to fulfill my destiny, I've been learning the art of self-defense from a book Mrs. Minnick gave me. I didn't go into the back room. Dad, could I practice my moves of self-defense on you so I can fulfill my destiny?" I gush. He smiles and pats my head.

"Sure, little lady. Give me all ya got." He laughs and blows smoke rings up into the air.

"Really? Okay!" I clasp my hands and melt in appreciation. Dad stands rooted to his spot, waiting for me. I run across the living room floor like a gazelle, then turn and face my father. As I prepare myself emotionally, physically, and spiritually, my heart races.

Precision, precision, precision is my mantra.

I fix my beady little eyes on my father's carotid artery and begin moving across the floor like a locomotive picking up speed.

"Tch tch tch tch, whoooo whooo!" is my siren song. I jump into the air, bring my arm back, and strike. "Hi-yaaahh!" I cry. Flesh meets flesh. Pop's eyes roll into the back of his head, and he slumps

to the ground, completely unconscious. I stand victorious! No longer a child but now an Amazonian artist capable of destroying the
father-enemy.

Each moment of life holds so many possibilities, doesn't it?

I could have done anything in those few minutes right before he
awoke and sniveled, "Jeesh, I didn't think you were gonna hit me so
hard."

In retrospect, I realize I should have gone for help or possibly even
called an ambulance when I thought I'd killed him. Somehow, none
of those choices occurred to me. Instead, I strode over to my father,
put my foot up onto his limp hip, raised my arms triumphantly, and
cried out, "Thank you, Mrs. Minnick!"

Matter Rearranged

People say I was an imaginative child.

Ridiculous! I was a scientist who was forced to use her bedroom as a laboratory due to lack of funding.

> *Query:* Can Pepsi-Cola create a mold that could slowly but efficiently manufacture a lifesaving serum to counteract a horrible, deadly virus moving through my hometown of Clayton, New York, located on the St. Lawrence River in the scenic Thousand Islands region, and possibly the world?

Procedure:
1. Take forty bottles of Pepsi-Cola.
2. Partially drink each bottle.
3. Measure the remaining contents of the bottles.
4. Label and date the bottles.
5. Line bottles up against the baseboard in bedroom.
6. Have this possibly true-life scenario reported by newscasters via satellite.

Conclusion: Pepsi-Cola is a mold medium that may contain lifesaving spores.

Results: Brother Tim mocks me by saying, "That mold looks like your teeth."

No Bunsen burner? No problem!

Query: How flammable is extremely flammable?

Procedure:
1. Create a mountain of cotton balls on pink vanity table.
2. Soak cotton balls in large bottle of nail polish remover.
3. Throw match.

Conclusion: Sister Cindi knows how to extinguish small fire with shirt while naked mother stands in hallway crying "Oh, dear! Oh, dear!" after getting out of tub.

Results: Sister Cindi tells me, "You are some kind of natural-born idiot."

No refrigeration? No impediment!

Query: Can the first successful human cryogenics experiment be simulated by total body immersion in a bathtub?

Procedure:
1. Substitute ice cubes for liquid nitrogen.
2. Make a lot of ice cubes and dump them in tub.
3. Strip down naked and get into tub.
4. Get out of tub.

Conclusion: Don't use untested materials on bare flesh.

Results: Nicknamed "Freeze Pop" by taunting siblings.

But honestly, I didn't let them bother me nor deter my will. Unperturbed and resolute, I decided to earn the respect of my family by proving my greatest theory of all.

Human matter can rearrange itself at will into anything within the animal, mineral, or spiritual kingdoms, and once rearranged, that human being will bear a mark to let other rearranged people know they belong to the club. I intuit the mark to be round and purplish, but I am open, because scientists are open. Like the fictional Dr. Jekyll, I decide to use myself as the test monkey. I hypothesize that since I have never witnessed my matter rearranged into a slug, a strawberry, or a sliver of starlight during my waking hours, it must happen during my sleep. I reason that my head will retain its Regi shape and visage, because I saw the movie *The Fly* with Vincent Price and he kept his head when his body turned into a fly. Art imitates life.

The idea that human matter can be rearranged isn't as abstract as it seems. The shamanistic religions have long believed that holy people can transform or project their essence into other matter. Once having gained the knowledge of another life form, the shaman reclaims his body and applies the knowledge for the good of his people.

Jesus rearranged his matter. Rising on the third day in his familiar visage, bearing the stigmata, he carried the promise of everlasting life to his faithful followers.

Even you and I know about rearranged matter. Think back to when you were on the cusp of puberty. Girls, you went to bed flat as a board. Boys, maybe you were cursed with a gherkin pickle nestled next to two kalamata olives between your legs. One morning, you young women awoke and had mounds on your chest. Boys, did you elongate? You didn't ask your body to do *that*, did you? Deoxyribonucleic acid has free will!

My plan of action is simple: keep a Polaroid camera next to my bedside and set my alarm for odd hours of the night such as 3:33, 1:19, or 5:07. I put my plan into action and set my alarm with my Polaroid camera at the ready. The alarm rings at 11:11. I am in Regi shape. The alarm *brrrings!* at 3:35, and still, I am in Regi shape. At 5:57, my shape is still Regi! No matter how fast I am, I cannot catch my body rearranged! I awake rearranged into Regi form before my brain can send a signal to my matter, before I can take a picture, show it to my parents, and gain the respect of my family that I so richly deserve. My brain is too smart for me! My scientist's hunch, my gut instinct, remains firm in its conviction, but I have absolutely no physical proof that my matter can rearrange itself. Damn you, DNA and your free will! Still, there is some lingering doubt. Oh, it isn't the science that is bothering me. I know that to be infallible. It is something else—something intangible. Then something happens, and it blows my theory wide open.

I awake one night without my alarm. It is really late, maybe eleven. I love waking late at night. My bedroom is directly above the kitchen where my parents continue to work after I go to bed. My mother's adding machine whirs as it tallies up the day's receipts from Carpenter's Grocery. My father fixes things with a hammer. The banging is followed by a very specific litany of swear words. His pipe smoke, Carter's Special Blend, wafts through the floorboards, and my room fills with hints of cherry and whiskey and tobacco. I can rock back to sleep listening to the river in the fall or summer. In the spring, I hear ice floes cracking apart or crashing into one another. On this night, however, everything is dark and quiet. This is the perfect scientific opportunity. I concentrate on sending my auric antennae out to snag any itinerant DNA floating in the air. My eyes are wide open. My antennae pulsate. I soon become aware of unfamiliar sounds that seem to be coming from my parents' room. Rhythmic, squeaky bed sounds and my mom moaning like she has a toothache. Wait a minute! The awful truth comes together in my mind. My parents are *doing it*!

It's.

So.

Gross.

I can hear her whispering, whimpering, and moaning in bed.

"Wait, wait," she says. *Wait for what?* But that isn't the worst part. My mother is *enjoying* doing it! What is she thinking? Every good Catholic knows the girl is not allowed to enjoy it. Only boys are allowed to enjoy it. My mother is going to hell! Mortified, I withdraw my antennae and pray for my mother's soul.

Hail Mary,

"Oh, yes . . . yes . . . yes."

full of Grace,

"Oh, baby."

the Lord is with thee.

Blessed art thou amongst women,

"Wait, wait . . ."

and blessed is the fruit of Thy womb, Jesus.

"Oh, oh, oh, oh, oh, ohhhhhh."

Holy Mary, Mother of God,

pray for us sinners, ESPECIALLY MY MOTHER,

now and at the hour of our death.

"Oh my God!"

Amen.

The shock of it knocks me out. The next thing I know, it is morning. It seems like a perfectly normal day—the birds are singing, the river is flowing, and the sun shines in the heavens. How could this be? Doesn't the universe know the world reversed its axis last night?

I get out of bed and pad down the beige vinyl carpet runner. Both my parents are in the kitchen. My mother is at the stove cooking my father's eggs and humming. My father is at the table reading the paper, smoking his pipe, and humming. I slip into my chair, pour myself a bowl of atomic neon-colored cereal, and add my customary twelve teaspoons of sugar. My mom comes over to the table and slips the eggs onto my father's plate. Dad drops his paper. I peek up. My parents' eyes meet. They smile at one another. They hum, and I see *it* on each of their necks. The mark! It *is* round and purplish! I intuited correctly! My parents prove my greatest theory of all for me because I am too young to do it. During sex, you get your matter rearranged.

One Man's Trash

Sunday is a day of rest for everyone in the Carpenter family except my mother. She calls Sunday "the day of the rest of it." Mom runs Carpenter's Grocery, our friendly family grocery store, Monday through Saturday from eight in the morning until eight at night, while my father spends the week as a traveling salesman. When two o'clock on Sunday rolls around, and the obligatory mass with Monsignor and the pot roast dinner are finally over, my mother wants a little time to herself away from us five kids and my father.

"Carl?" she calls to my father from the kitchen.

"Yuh?" he replies and sucks air through his teeth.

"May I speak to you for a moment?" she gently requests.

"Ah, jeez." Dropping the Sunday paper, he slowly slinks into the kitchen.

My diminutive mother stands there, hands on her hips and daggers in her eyes.

"Carl, don't you want to do something with your children today?"

"I *am* doing something, Jo. I'm reading the paper in the same room they're fightin' in."

"Charming. No, Carl, I mean *do* something outside of the house.

Just you and them—all five of them for the entire afternoon. Hmm?"

"Aww, jeesh, Jo, don't get yer dandruff up." Looking down, he hitches his britches and hollers, "C'mon kids, let's go for a walk!"

We whoop and scramble out the front door. Standing on the corner of James Street and Mary Street, Dad's long, lanky body hovers over us.

"Kids, if I've told ya once, I've told ya a hundred times: one man's trash is another man's treasure. Never forget that. So, while we're out walkin' around town, keep your eyes peeled to the ground. Any half-smoked butts or loose change you find, pass 'em over to yer old man."

We morph into human Geiger counters, clicking and scanning the ground for Camels and quarters until my father's pockets bulge. That isn't all we do, though. Sometimes we stand on the municipal dock and watch people fish. If we're lucky, somebody steps on a nail. Other times, we go to Mercier's Beach, where all the Catholic kids learn to flail, swim, or drown. Pop stands on the beach and pretends to be a whale, flapping his flipper arms. We're barnacles attached to his neck. Swimming to the buoy and back to shore, he plants his tail fin in the sand, shakes us off, and blows water out his piehole. Some Sundays we walk around town, looking in our neighbors' windows. Hours later, with the sun setting on the St. Lawrence River, we return home to my mother's tender embrace and Jell-O cooling in a bowl on the countertop.

"Isn't Jell-O supposed to be cold, Mom? And jiggle?" Mary asks timidly.

"This is Jell-O *juice*. Be grateful for that, kids, because if you think I have time to put that Jell-O into the refrigerator so it can jiggle, you can just jiggle yourself right out of here!" Her voice sounds like a cat being boiled.

Not all Sundays are full of sweet-smelling roses, though. Sometimes two o'clock comes at one thirty and Mom has a twitch in her eye.

"Carl?" is the call from the kitchen.

"Yuh?"

"May I speak to you for a moment?"

Dad sucks air in through his teeth. "Ah, jeez." He slumps into the kitchen.

"Don't you want to do something with your children today?"

"Not really, Jo, no."

"Oh, I think you do, Carl. I think you *do*."

"Well, whaddya expect me to do with 'em?"

"I don't know, Carl, but if you don't get those children out of here, I'm afraid I . . . I . . . ." and here she clutches at her heart and sobs, "I'm afraid I might lure them into a sack with Ho Hos and Twinkies and then put a rock in that sack and drown them in the river! Now please, Carl, do it! I'm desperate!" Tears stream down her face.

"Jeez, Jo, honey, don't get yer dandruff up."

Dad looks down and rubs his neck. He hitches his britches.

"C'mon, kids, let's go have some fun!" My father, Carl Henry Carpenter, spells fun T-R-O-U-B-L-E.

We're standing on the corner of James Street and Mary Street. Dad's long, lanky body hovers over us, and his eyes gleam. The shovel he calls his hand reaches deep into his pocket. He pulls out the car keys and gives them a jangle.

"Hey kids, wanna go for a drive?" he leans in and whispers.

Our pupils dilate as we run to the red, rusted Bonneville station wagon with the wood paneling duct-taped to the side. Scraping open the back door, we pile into the backseat, which is always down and covered with ratty quilts just in case we go by a good drive-in movie. We crawl over one another until we resemble a ball of worms on a cold, wet morning.

My father saunters to the driver's side, pulls open the door, and slides behind the wheel. He lights a half-smoked Camel and blows smoke rings. *Bwah, wah, wah, wah.* Then he turns the key. The car spits, lunges, coughs, and backfires. Dad's hand is on the dash, cajoling and cooing the car to life.

"Come on, baby, come on, baby." Spit. Cough. Backfire. "Be good to Daddy, be good to Daddy, be good, be good." The engine purrs. "Who loves ya, baby? Daddy loves ya. That's who loves ya," he says as he caresses the dash.

The radio clicks on. It's always the same music all Sunday drive long—a spy song, saxophone like a siren and a slap shot on the drums. *Doo doot, doo doot, doo doo doot doot.*

Magically, a chocolate-brown fedora hat appears on the passenger side of the front seat. Dad picks it up and covers that Carpenter hair—always black, wavy, and pomaded until it's flammable. His hand goes to the wand on the steering column. Before he shifts out of park, he turns to look at each one of us.

"Now, kids, when you're out for a Sunday drive, it's important to observe all the traffic rules and regulations. *All* the traffic rules and regulations, kids. Never forget that."

He reverses onto Mary Street. Once in drive, the car points itself to the stop sign there on the corner of James and Mary.

The turn signal sings *Blink, blink. Blink, blink.* The radio pumps *Doo doot, doo doot, doo doo doot doot.* The adventure begins.

We hang a right on James Street, driving past St. Mary's Catholic Church, past the rectory, and past Mrs. Fitzgerald's chestnut tree until we get to the one traffic light in town with the arching neon sign that reads *Thank you for visiting the beautiful Thousand Islands region.*

"We wait at the red light," Father reminds us. "Always observe the traffic rules and regulations, kids; rules and regulations. Never forget that." Smoke rings circle the globe of his head.

The light turns green, and the car slides through the intersection. James Street becomes Route 12. We move away from town and drive by Clayton Central School and Mr. Frick's ice cream stand with the twenty-foot Plaster of Paris vanilla-and-chocolate-twist ice cream cone out front. We hold our breath passing the cemetery until we see the white house on the other side. Dad blows smoke rings. His fingers tap the wheel to the beat. We peek over the front seat. Hold our breath. Wish on a star. The turn signal sings *Blink, blink. Blink, blink.*

We turn right onto "Roller Coaster Road" and start to pick up speed. Twenty miles per hour. Thirty miles per hour. Seventy, eighty-two miles per hour, then two hundred miles per hour! The car soars into the air and slams down. Again and again, we soar and slam, soar and slam. In the backseat, our fingers are up each other's noses, feet in faces, arms and legs flying out of the windows. We're spaghetti twirling around in a little kid's mouth. Then the wood paneling duct-taped to the side of the car flies straight out and becomes wings! The car is Pegasus, and, like Icarus, we soar to the sun only to drop down to the paved sea. Dad slams on the brakes at the stop sign. Our heads hit the back of the front seat. We uncross our eyes, lift our heads, and cry out, "DO IT AGAIN!"

"Rules and regulations, kids. Rules and regulations. Never forget that." *Bwah, wah, wah, wah.*

We turn left onto a hitherto unseen and unknown road. The car passes an invisible line. The sky blackens. Green ooze bubbles up from the earth. Now the flies are as big as hummingbirds. An acrid stench fills the air. Our nostrils flare. Our eyes tear. A metallic taste lingers on our tongues, and our skin begins to slough off. We're quiet in the back seat. Could we hope it? Dare it? Could it possibly be? Yes! We *are* going to the dump! A mile down the road, the car pulls over and kills its own engine.

My father gets out, throws his cigarette to the ground, grinds it out with his heel, and hitches his pants.

"Kids, let's go shoppin'!" We pile out and stand on the precipice of a putrid paradise. Dante's *Inferno* has NOTHING on the Clayton town dump! There are all kinds of good stuff down there! Cars nobody wants anymore, furniture nobody wants anymore, appliances nobody wants anymore, and possibly relatives nobody wants anymore. There are rats as big as schnauzers and female dogs with so many litters their teats could double for cake frosting decorating funnels. Smoke spews and billows from burning piles of rubber. My father extends his arms, inhales deeply, and throws back his head.

"Ah, life! Now, kids, if I've told ya once, I've told ya a hundred times. One man's trash is another man's treasure."

We pick our way down the path. My brothers leave to shoot rocks at cans. My sisters and I stick with the old man. The four of us carefully pick our way around piles of petroleum products given to spontaneous combustion. Dad finds a doll with one eye hanging out and one arm dangling down. Mary and Cindi fight me over the doll.

"I want it! I want it! I'm the baby! I should get it!" I whine.

"You always get everything. I'm the middle girl. All I ever get is the blame!" Mary yells back at me.

"I'm the eldest. It's mine by birthright!" Cindi chimes in.

"Now, girls, don't fight. Look around. There's plenty of good stuff down here for everyone."

At the end of the afternoon, we all have some treasure to take home.

My father has a television set. A television set is full of mystery—it's got bubble glass, front knobs that control the horizontal and vertical hold, and tubes that hum and glow when turned on. The real wood console tells you it's not just a television but a piece of furniture. We all help carry it up the path and load it into the station wagon. On the way home, Dad observes all the traffic rules and regulations.

The car cuts out in our driveway. We sneak the television out of the car and in through the front door, trying to drag it into the living room. My mother sees us coming in, and her face implodes.

"Carl, what are you doing?"

"Jo, if I've told ya once, I've told ya a hundred times. One man's trash is—"

"This woman's junk!" she interrupts and stomps away.

But we all see the Jell-O juice cooling on the counter. Everything is going to be okay in a little while, just like always.

We take the TV into the living room and put it with our other five television sets. Now we have six—two towers of TVs. The three on the right have sound that works but no picture. The three on the left have a picture that works but no sound.

———————————

Dad tunes into the same thing every Sunday: a football game, Minnesota Fats (the trick billiards player), and a John Wayne movie. All three of the pictures are on simultaneously, but the soundtrack of each show is turned up or down depending on my father's fancy. "Reg, turn down the game and turn up the movie, 'cause I think John Wayne's gonna kiss Maureen O'Hara. I don't wanna miss that."

I am the original remote control.

Mom joins us at six o'clock refreshed and calm like we knew she would be. The evening begins when we gather to watch *Mutual of Omaha's Wild Kingdom*. At seven, we marvel at Walt Disney's *Wonderful World of Color*, then ride horses with Hoss during *Bonanza*, laugh through the really big shoe of Ed Sullivan, and, finally, sing with Carol Burnett, "I'm so glad we had this time together, just to have a laugh or sing a song."

Mom makes a big bowl of popcorn. When she comes back into the living room, my father pats the couch, winks, and sees only my mother.

"Who loves ya, baby? Daddy loves ya, that's who loves ya." Dad's arm slides around Mom, and her head finds his shoulder. The room fills with the sound of crunching popcorn and slurps of Jell-O juice.

We finish with a thriller—*Mission Impossible*. Jim Phelps, the master spy, always accepts his mission.

The day ends as it began—kneeling next to the bed we got from the Clayton town dump. The headboard reads *Bobby slept here*. Clutching my one-armed, one-legged doll, I pray that next week, two o'clock comes at one thirty and Mom has a twitch in her eye.

Mrs. Carter

The carnival we call summer is winding down like a tired top. The whitecaps on the St. Lawrence River settle down at night like chickens roosting at sunset. The marbles circle and hopscotch game adorning our front sidewalk has been swept away. The summer streets usually filled with cars and boats and tourists are back to normal with just the residents running the stop signs.

It's September 3, and tomorrow is the first day of school. I have to take a bath and wash my hair, which my mother will ruin by combing. She'll add to my torture by making me go to bed early. She's sewn me a new dress and bought me a pair of special-order shoes that squeak, some No. 2 pencils, a composition notebook, and a box of 24 Crayola crayons. She wraps a quarter for my weekly meal ticket in a Kleenex. I tuck it and my lucky rabbit's foot into the pocket of my dress. I'm eight years old and about to start third grade.

Clayton Central School was built on a big, grassy, rolling plot of land right outside of town. It's a mile walk from my house. On that first day of school, and every one after it, I skip up James Street until I meet some friends. It doesn't take long for us to become a pack of kids all moving together like a school of fish toward the shores of higher learning. We enter the dark corridors with floors that gleam and smell of wax. I walk straight past the gymnasium and office and down the hallway.

My teacher, Mrs. Carter, is standing in the doorway of our classroom. She's very tall with dark hair and silvery sparkling cat glasses. The belt on her dress is cinched so tight her belly pops out underneath it. She has pointy black flat shoes. She must have washed her hair the night before too and put it up in curlers because one of the pink plastic curlers is still in her hair. As I stand at the entryway to our classroom, her smile beams down at me. "Good morning, Regi," she says, and suddenly, it is.

As she walks me to my desk at the back of the first row, I mention she has a hole in her stockings. "Wonderful! Now my fat has somewhere to go on vacation!"

I'm in love.

One by one, all the kids in my class take their seats. Once we're all here and attendance is over, Debbie McGrath raises her hand.

"My grandma has a big poochy belly like you do, Mrs. Carter."

"Children," Mrs. Carter explains as she cups her belly like an egg, "this is not a poochy belly; it's a pouch. Who can tell me what mammal has a pouch? Whomever answers that correctly shall receive a kiss." My hand shoots up and waves like a puppy's tail.

"I know, I know," I stammer.

After I answer, I catch her hand-blown kiss and put it in my pocket for later.

Every morning after attendance and lunch count, we stand and say the Pledge of Allegiance. Then someone squawks morning announcements through the loudspeaker and our day begins. We have a strict daily routine. We study something, have a midmorning snack, have art, music, or gym, study something else, eat lunch, have recess, have reading time with Mrs. Carter, and then study something else, and at 3:15, we get to go home.

I notice right away there's something different about Mrs. Carter from the other teachers I've had. Instead of using her pointer and scowling at us, she smiles and sings and teaches with games! One particular morning in October, she is teaching us the mathematical symbols for *more than* and *less than*.

"This is the symbol for *more than*," says Mrs. Carter. She draws a > on the board in white chalk and uses colored chalk to give it an eye and a mouth. It looks like a fish's head. "If the fish is swimming forward, children, that means there is *more* fish for us to eat." Then she draws a hook in the fish's mouth. "That's *more than*. BUT—" and here she raises her hand in the air and does an impersonation of the rusted Tin Man holding his ax, "if the fish is swimming away from you," she continues and draws the < symbol to make it look like a fish swimming in the opposite direction, "that means there will be *less* fish." She draws the hook, but it doesn't catch the fish. We all nod our heads in understanding.

"Let's practice."

Mrs. Carter writes the numbers 1 and 2 on the board.

"Class, is one more or less than two? Put on fish faces and lean right if it's more and left if it's less."

We all suck in our cheeks to look like fish and lean left in our chairs. Mrs. Carter smiles.

"Good. Now, is thirteen more or less than twelve?"

We all lean right. She keeps writing numbers on the board while we lean from one side to the other like metronomes. We're leaning and laughing so hard that one boy falls off his chair and breaks his tooth. When he leaves the room to go to the nurse, she asks us, "Does he have more or less teeth now than he had this morning?" We laugh and lean left.

When it's time to learn our multiplication tables, she puts on the record to the Bunny Hop. We sing and hop, "One times one is one hop. One times two is two hops," until the bunny hops so much that it knows one times any number is that number itself.

There is a special helper every week who gets to deliver the attendance and lunch count to the office and run errands for Mrs. Carter if she needs it. My favorite errand is picking up mimeographs for math. The office ladies hand-crank the mimeographs off and hand them to me. They're still warm, and my hands turn blue as the ink rubs off onto them, but it's the smell of ether as it fills my nostrils and makes me loopy that I really love.

Tuesdays bring Mr. Connor and music class. Mr. Connor is a short round man whose arms swing as he pounds the piano passionately. He stamps his foot and sings with his head thrown back. We warm up by singing "The Halls of Montezuma" and "The Erie Canal." While playing a record of "Flight of the Bumblebee," Mr. Connor moves a stuffed bumblebee on a stick around the room and lands on us as if we were flowers. Mr. Connor loves music. When he plays us records, his eyes close and he gets lost between the notes. I get a solo to sing in the Christmas concert. Mrs. Carter tells me I "sing like a bird." My mother makes me a dress for the concert and hand-sews moons and stars on the bottom. I feel like I am singing on a cloud.

On Wednesday mornings, our usual routine is interrupted when Professor DiStefano wheels his cart in to teach us about art. I like art because the paste tastes good. One day, he asks us to draw a cow and then a dog and then a cat and finally a tree. Then he comes around to look at our work. When he gets to my desk, Professor DiStefano holds my paper up, squints his eyes, and flips the paper upside down and then right side up while moving it back and forth a couple of times. The next art class, I write the name of whatever he asks us to draw underneath it because obviously he can't tell the difference between a perfectly drawn cat or cow. After the professor leaves one day, Mrs. Carter says, "Always color outside the lines, children; it is much more interesting." She takes out her red lipstick and applies it around her mouth. It looks like she's just eaten a piece of fresh cherry pie.

Gym class is on Thursdays. Mrs. Carter tells us how lucky we are because we get to do gymnastics this year—especially the trampoline, which she excelled in as a girl. We make a circle around the trampoline and Mrs. Bazinet teaches us how to "spot" one another. That means if you go crazy when you're jumping and bounce off the trampoline, someone will put their arms out to signal where the safe spot is to land so you can crush them and save yourself. During my turn, Mrs. Bazinet keeps telling me to jump higher and higher. "What time is it, Regi?" she asks me. I boing up into the air to see the clock at the top of the wall. My teeth hurt when I land and I think I am going to pee myself, but I can't stop. It's too much fun. *Boing! Boing! BO-ING!* I am going higher and higher. "Mrs. Bazinet, it's ten thirty!" She smiles, and my turn is over.

"Work and play some each day," Mrs. Carter tells us. On Friday afternoons, we wash the tops of our desks and organize them for the next week. After desk inspection, we play our favorite game, Hide the Eraser. One kid is "It" and goes into the hall while the rest of us hide the eraser somewhere impossible to find. It's usually in the same spot each week because it's such a good spot. Once the eraser is safely tucked away and out of sight, "It" returns and begins searching for the eraser. We give "It" help by shouting temperature clues. As "It" moves closer or farther away from the eraser, we shout out varying degrees of hot for close and cold for not.

"Use your scientific vocabulary, children. Use geography," Mrs. Carter insists.

"You are in a glacier freezing to death at the Arctic Circle!" Susie chokes out as "It" moves way off base.

"Very good. Very good," says Mrs. Carter.

"You are in molten lava from an active volcano in Hawaii!" Kendra cries as "It" inches closer to the secreted artifact.

"Excellent!" Mrs. Carter responds.

"You are frying up to a crisp on the Equator!" Freddie yells.

"Masterful!" she coos and hands "It" the eraser.

Mrs. Carter is a firefighter. I discover this during a spelling test. We're being tested on the "*i* before *e* except after *c* but mostly you just have to remember it" rule. I'm excited because I've practiced all week long to get a 100 percent. During the test, she says the word, puts it in a sentence, and then repeats the word. "Believe. I can't believe you told a lie. Believe." Once we're finished with all ten words, we pass them forward from the back of the row to the front. Mrs. Carter is waiting for the papers to come forward when she asks the girl sitting at the front of my row to hand in her test.

"I did hand it in, Mrs. Carter," she answers.

"Are you sure, dear?" Mrs. Carter asks, looking through the pile of papers.

"I am absolutely sure," the girl says confidently.

Then a strange thing happens: the room starts to heat up. The lie that girl just told is a spark that shoots out her mouth and starts a fire in our classroom.

"Are you sure, dear?" Mrs. Carter asks again.

"I handed it in," the girl insists. Like magic, the spark flies out of her mouth and lands in the mouth of the kid next to her.

"I saw her hand it in, Mrs. Carter," he declares. Suddenly, the spark flies to another nearby kid, and he too insists that he saw her hand the paper in. Then the room begins to crackle as the flames of "Me too" and "I saw her do it" spark. Everybody is shouting that they saw her hand the spelling paper in. The flames of deception lick our faces. The blaze makes it back to me and I say it too even though I sit so far in the back I couldn't possibly have seen her hand it in. As we file past her to go to lunch, Mrs. Carter has a very sad look on her face. After recess, we run in and sit down with our hands folded and ankles crossed to show Mrs. Carter we're ready for her to read to us. Instead of holding a book in her hand as usual, she is standing behind her desk holding a wadded-up piece of paper. We sit quietly.

"I found this spelling test stuffed in her desk." She points to the girl's desk. "Those of you who said you saw her hand it in were very sadly mistaken. You all get an F." She stares at each one of us in turn, and we understand the lesson she is teaching us isn't about spelling. Instead of reading to us that day, we have to sit with our heads on our desks.

Mrs. Carter reads to us every day after recess, which is when we play deadly games of dodgeball and perfect the art of swinging until we almost barf. When Mrs. Carter reads, she puts funny expressions in her voice and raises her eyebrows and makes silly faces. She reads us *Oh, the Places You'll Go!* by that kooky Dr. Seuss. (Dr. Seuss must not have ever been to Clayton, because he never mentions that one of the places we might go is prison or communion.) She also reads us *The Velveteen Rabbit* and *The Lion, the Witch and the Wardrobe*. I like *The Velveteen Rabbit* because it reminds me of my stuffed pink elephant and *The Lion, the Witch and the Wardrobe* because sometimes my brothers lock me in the closet and that would be cool if I could escape out the other side. But my favorite book by far is *Charlotte's Web*. Charlotte's as good a speller as I am, and Fern is so nice that I think if she was real she could be a friend of mine. Near the end of the book when Charlotte summons all her strength and waves good-bye to Wilbur with one of her front legs, I cry without making any sounds. Tears roll down my face as I drop my head down to my arms. When Charlotte dies, I am thinking about my Grandma Carpenter who died before I ever met her and my cat last year who caught a cold and asked to be let out and never came back in and the old woman next door that I used to deliver milk to and talk with while she fed her cats and my father who's always in the hospital and Old Yeller. Mrs. Carter keeps reading as she slowly walks to my desk and rubs my back. Later she whispers, "I know, dear. I know."

In January, I get sick with a fever that doesn't go away and I miss a lot of school. I'm too dizzy to walk up the stairs to my bedroom, so most of the time I lay on a blanket on the couch while my mother rubs my body down with witch hazel. Our family physician, Dr. Fawkes, makes daily house calls. He's taken a hypocrite's oath instead of the Hippocratic one. He's trying to kill me with penicillin. I over-hear my mother on the phone telling Mrs. Carter she doesn't know when I'll be back in school. The days are long, and I am in and out of sleep and sweat. I just lie there while my family bustles around me. One afternoon, my mother combs my hair and helps me change my nightgown. That afternoon, I have a visitor. Mrs. Carter has get-well letters from everyone in my class. While sitting on the edge of my bed, she reads me every letter and shows me the pictures my friends have drawn. Not one of them has labeled their cats or dogs or flow-ers, but I know what they are anyway. Soon after that, I start feeling better and go back to school.

The year moves forward like a freighter toward the sea. I have to wear glasses. I get chubby. Once I can see the board, my grades go up, but my spirits go down when the kids call me "four eyes" and "fatty, fatty, two-by-four" on the playground. Back in the classroom, Mrs. Carter makes me do my homework over if I do a sloppy job. She makes me practice my cursive *v*'s and *u*'s until she can tell the difference between them. She tells me I look beautiful when I come to school in ten different shades of red. She thinks that naturally curly hair is a blessing and not a curse and wishes she had it. She tells me to hold on and things will get better, and they do. Mrs. Carter is strange and kind and funny. By the end of third grade, she has taught me much more than math and reading and good penmanship.

On the last day of third grade, I stand at the doorway after everyone has left and take one last glance at Mrs. Carter. She and I share a look, and I want to tell her all the things that I'm thinking, like *Why do I have to wear glasses?* and *Why do the kids make fun of my curly hair?* and *Why do fathers and mothers fight?* and *Why do I like to read more than anything else?* and *Have you ever noticed that the frosting on a cupcake looks like a toupee?* and *Isn't music beautiful?* and *I will never have as nice a teacher as you,* but I don't say anything. I just look at her with all those thoughts in my head. She looks at me. Her smile is like a spotlight. She says, "I know, dear. I know." And so I leave school to play hopscotch and marbles with my sister.

God is Love

I like living on Mary Street even though we are hungry sometimes, and both our parents walk out after having a fight with one another and we don't know if they are coming back, and we have to scatter like marbles to avoid my father who pops off like a cork after we say the rosary. I can work around those things because the yellow canary in the golden cage in the kitchen sings along to the warped records on the portable hi-fi, and the hot yeasted rolls my father makes in the winter taste so good, and the skunk mittens my mother knits me pretend to talk, and our dog Snoopy smells good, and I love my sister Mary.

There are three bedrooms for the seven of us. My brothers, Dave and Tim, have the back bedroom. My parents sleep in the middle, and Cindi, Mary, and I share the biggest bedroom in the front facing the river. Cindi is the oldest, so she gets her own bed. Mary and I sleep together in the double bed next to the pink vanity and dresser. At the end of the day, Mary and I lie in bed and talk about Barbie dolls and worms before we turn over to go to sleep. Mary sleeps like a log, but I don't. I wake up at night and watch the shadows on the wall and hear the river creeping up to the shore. Some nights, every shadow is a nightmare. I wake Mary up to help me.

"There's something on the dresser, and it's staring at me. I think it's moving. I think it's a mean clown," I whisper and tremble. Mary sits up and looks.

"Nah," she says. "It's your teddy bear. Come here and cuddle with me. It's okay."

When Mom buys the store and we move to James Street, Cindi, Mary, and I still share a bedroom. Cindi gets single bed privileges because of her seniority, so Mary and I share a bunk bed. We still have the same dresser and pink vanity, which sit next to my Barbie dolls and Trolls with a collapsible house. Mary is getting "mature" now, and I start to notice she is changing. She has magical powers of perception. When we play with the Ouija board, she interprets the secrets of the spirits. "The spirits want you to do my chores on Saturday. They say you will get better Christmas presents if you do," she divines.

Mary and I do lots of chores every Saturday morning. We change the sheets on all the beds, sweep the floors, scrub sinks, pick up dog poop from behind the couch, and fold the wrinkled laundry. We empty my father's ashtrays and clean his corncob pipes, do the dishes, and peel potatoes for supper. It takes us hours to clean the house, but we like it. The vacuum is our microphone, and we stop to rest by lolling around on the beds, messing up what we've just straightened. We catch sunlight in our cupped palms. Mary vacuums up the spiderwebs in the corner of each room because I am scared of the spiders. Some nights, I wake up thinking about the spiders. I climb up to Mary's bed and accidentally wake her up.

"Do you think the spiders will climb out the vacuum hose and come and get us because we sucked up their family?" I whisper.

"Nah, they can't climb the stairs that well," she says and flicks back her comforter so I can climb in.

———————————

Mary is smarter than me in ways I don't understand. For example, she always knows where the matching card is when we play Concentration. She can see the cards even though they are turned downward and remember where they are after looking at them just once. She can remember numbers she's heard someone say. She can do many things I can't, but there are some things she can't figure out at all.

My father dishes out the mashed potatoes after the blessing. Someone spills their milk, and we robotically lift our plates as Mom sops it up. He bellows, "Do ya think milk grows on trees?!" I know to keep my head down, but Mary incites him by speaking before being spoken to.

She says something provocative like "Please pass the butter." Without warning, his chair is thrown back and it hits the floor. Mary jumps up just in time to start running. They are playing a twisted game of Duck, Duck, Goose. I shut my eyes or fall to the floor under the table next to the dog so I don't have to see what I can hear is happening.

"I didn't do anything! I didn't do it!" she whimpers when his hand connects to the side of her head.

Smack!

Why doesn't she just be quiet? I think. *She should know better by now.*

Thwap!

I am going to be perfect. I will be perfect, and then nothing bad will ever happen to me. If I am perfect, I will be safe.

———————————

Eventually, Mary and I get separate rooms. Now I have privacy so I can play secretary with a long black stocking on my head and do some important science experiments like growing mold in Pepsi bottles to see if I can make an immunization that might save the world or something else that may change the course of history.

It's Sunday afternoon, and the store is closed. My mom is in the tub. My father is downstairs watching the game. I am in my room pouring the entire contents of a bottle of nail polish remover onto a mountain of cotton balls on my pink vanity. The nail polish remover drips down the side of the vanity and pools on the floor. *How flammable is "extremely flammable"?* I wonder as I toss a lighted match onto the mountain of cotton balls. *Whoosh!* Extremely flammable turns out to be exceedingly flammable. The fire rushes upward in colors of red and yellow before it finds its feet and starts running down the vanity leg and to the floor. The flames are spraying up from the floor like geysers. I step on them to put them out, but fire is such a fast runner that I can't catch up. The hairbrush on my vanity begins to melt as the flames admire themselves in the mirror. All that running makes them hungry, so they lick my walls like a kid with an ice cream cone. Black smoke billows into the air. I stand still as the fire runs up the walls, runs down to the floor, and somersaults toward my bed.

"Fire! Fire!" I scream and then stand there completely frozen. No one comes. "Fire! Fire!" I scream again. Cindi, the quick-thinking one in the family, runs in from the front bedroom, whips off her striped shirt, and snuffs out the flames while my naked, dripping wet mother runs out of the bathroom, stands on the beige vinyl carpet runner in the hallway, wrings her hands, and whispers, "Oh, dear. Oh, dear." My room looks like charred meat. The walls are seared, the floor is scorched, and the smoke is overstaying its welcome. My dad smells the fire and follows the smoke. Once he sees my room, he is hell-bent on revenge.

"Who did it?" he thunders as fire and brimstone surround him. I stand alone in my room looking at my father.

I could have said so many things in that moment, like "I'm sorry. I didn't know that would happen" or "I did it," or I could have pulled a fake-out and said, "Did what?" I could have thrown myself upon my father's mercy. Instead, I lie. "Mary did it," I say. As soon as he has exacted my confession, he turns and calls her name. She is downstairs in the kitchen making a sandwich. He goes down the stairs, and I can hear the *zzzz* of his belt being pulled through his belt loops. There is the sound of chairs hitting the floor and the light steps of Mary's feet and the heavy steps of Dad's feet as they play their demented Duck, Duck, Goose game. He catches her, and I hear the smack of the belt against her bare flesh. Each time the strap hits her, I get a welt on my leg.

"I didn't do it! I didn't do it!" she cries.

I feel her forty lashes. I am a Judas. I want to be good. I *want* to be perfect. I skulk slowly downstairs and face my father. My lips feel chapped, and my hands are cold.

"I did it. She didn't do it. I'm sorry."

Dad stops, belt in midair. His mouth hangs open, and he lets go of Mary. She rushes off to lick her wounds. My mother tells me I am such a good girl for telling the truth. I don't get the belt. Instead, my mother tucks me in that night. Her love and kindness are the worst punishment I could get.

Mary has a heart of gold. She forgives me, and we go back to being best friends playing marbles on the sidewalk next to our front porch. It's a beautiful summer day. One of those clear-blue-sky, cars-whiz-by, horns-toot-and-birds-squawk days. We've each got a pile of penny candy—Mary Janes, Fireballs, Lemon Drops, Tootsie Rolls, Black Crows—and a pouch filled with glass marbles. I like the clear ones with the ribbons of color running through the middle, and Mary likes the solid-colored ones. The marbles clack against one another as the shooters and cat's eyes move position inside the circle. The circle is three feet wide in diameter. We each have three marbles in the ring, including our lucky cat's eye. The object of the game is to knock the other person's marbles out of the circle. Once you do that, their marbles are yours and you can trade them back for pieces of bubble gum or Tootsie Rolls. It's my turn. I flick my midnight-blue shooter with flecks of gold in it. Mary's shooter is milky white. Hers looks like the day and mine the night. To shoot, I lie flat on the ground and line my eye up with the marbles. I flick the shooter off my thumb. It rolls into the circle and scatters Mary's marbles. They sound like knitting needles as they click against one another. One rolls out of the circle. I snatch it up and put it in my pouch.

"Ha, ha," I taunt. Mary shoots her shooter but only succeeds in knocking one of her own marbles out of the circle. I grab it. "Finders keepers!" I say. We continue flicking our shooters in the circle. As we play, the circle begins to look like the night sky and the marbles like the constellations. With each flick of a shooter, the circle on the sidewalk widens, and it's as if I am peering down a well and into the waters of the universal night sky despite being on my sidewalk on a sunny summer day. The marbles are constantly shifting stars.

Flick the shooter, see the night sky!

It's Mary's turn. She flicks her solid white shooter, and the marbles reposition themselves inside the circle, making Orion's Belt, the Little Dipper, and Cassiopeia. The circle widens, and it's as if I am looking into the night sky at the dawning of life.

Flick the shooter, see the constellations as only those in the beginning of time did!

I flick my shooter, and the marbles look like the Little Dipper.

"Your turn," she says.

Flick the shooter, understand the mystery of the universe!

The marbles keep moving and shifting their positions. Horns toot. People pass by and greet us by name. I hear the whirring of bicycle tires and buzzing flies. She gets one of mine. I capture her lucky cat's eye.

I flick my own shooter out of the circle. She catches it and hands it back to me. "Try again; do over," she says. I shoot. Mary's remaining marbles scatter and roll out of the circle.

"I win!" I shout triumphantly, lifting my eyes up to the midday sky. The sun is bright, and there are no clouds. Seagulls are flying in a circle above me. The sky is so open, the sun so warm. Crickets rub their legs together, warming up for their midday dance. Flies buzz around our heads, and passing cars beep their horns in courtesy to jaywalking squirrels. People passing by greet us by name. There is a peace and stillness from the sky that floats through the air and takes up space inside of me.

Just then, I hear a voice say, "You are not the center of the universe."

"Did you say something, Mary?" I ask.

"Nah, you're imagining things."

I put all the marbles in my pouch and head into the house to gloat over my winnings. As my hand touches the doorknob, I hear the same quiet voice say, "God is love."

I turn back to Mary. She is sitting alone in the dirt, picking a scab on her leg, and looking into the now-empty marbles circle. I ask, "Wanna play again? You can use my shooter this time."

Love is War

My daddy was in WWII,
went in at eighteen, came out at twenty-two.
Married my mama in Cal-i-for-ni-a;
both lived to rue and bless the day.

My father's love affair with my mother started two years before he met her:

It was October 1939. I was seventeen and a junior in high school when a bunch of us guys from Clayton—Rory, Milt, Sullivan, Natali, and Pete—decided we wanted to join up in the National Guard. I mean, where else could ya make a buck on a Saturday morning just for walking around? That's what we thought. So the lot of us walk across town to the Chevy dealership on Riverside Drive. Cliff Good owned the dealership, and he was the captain of the National Guard in Watertown. Cliff's got his head stuck under the hood of a Chevy, smokin' and fixin' a gas line.

"Hey, Cliff, do you think we could join up in the Guard?" I ask him.

He pulls his head out from under the hood, looks us up and

down, takes a smoke, and says, "Ah yut." That was that. See, he knew our people.

The next Saturday, we hitchhike our way to Watertown and Armory Square. Cliff puts us through our paces.

Hup, two, three, four,
hup, two, three, four,
hup, two, three, four;
at ease, men.

We don't have any guns, so when he orders "Bear arms!" we just roll up our sleeves and show each other our biceps. This was before the country had gone into weapon production, Reg. Nobody was training with guns. Everybody was trainin' with broomsticks. So we finish our maneuvers, sweep off the square, get our buck, and take the money home to our mothers. The whole thing was just a lot of fun. That's the way we looked at it, a whole lot of fun. But in October of 1940, when I was a senior, we got called into action.

The National Guard was rolled into the Army, and I was put into the 184th battalion. I was shipped out to Alabama for basic, then to Oklahoma, and finally, in 1941, I ended up in Riverside, California, at the big base out there. California was where I met the person who would change my life—Jimmy Forbes!

Jimmy was a great guy and a lotta fun. He and I took to one another right off the bat. Jimmy called California the land of "opportunity," better known as . . . "girls." Jimmy had a real way with the women. One day, he comes to me and says, "Carl, I was wonderin' if you could help me out a little bit."

"What can I do for you, Jim?"

"Well, I'm going out with these two sisters, and it's a little bit more than I can handle. You think you could go out with the younger sister? She's a real live wire."

I put my hand over my heart and say, "Jim, you know I'd do anything for my country."

So I start going out with the younger sister. We're going out for a coupla months, dancin' and the movies and whatnot, when she comes to me and says, "Carl, I can't go out with you anymore."

I'm shocked 'cause I thought things were goin' pretty good. "Why not?" I ask.

She says, "Well, my husband's coming back from Hawaii next week. I think I better spend some time with him."

Go figure. So I told Jimmy about it. He says, "Carl, plenty more fish in the ocean. I'll take care of ya."

That's how I met your mother.

> *My mama was just sweet sixteen,*
> *wore bobby sox, her face was squeaky clean.*
> *My daddy fell in love right away;*
> *it was sixty-one years, give or take a day.*

The minute I saw Josephine, I said, "Jackpot!" I knew she was the one.

Your mother was standing under a movie marquee for *The Mask of Zorro*. She was bee-uuu-ti-ful—just a little slip of a thing. No bigger than a minute. Her hair was the color of wheat and waved down to her shoulders. Her skin was like a china doll. Her eyes, though, I kept staring at them. I couldn't tell if they were cornflower blue or spring green. I still don't know. Did you know that the first time I put my hands around your mother's waist, they went around two times? Yes, they did.

Well, I started seeing your mother as much as I could. I hitch-hiked from Riverside to Anaheim every chance I got. Went AWOL a couple of times, got thrown into the pokey, too—don't look at my discharge papers, Reg. It was worth it, though. Your mother was worth it.

In April, we got word that we were getting shipped out to the

Pacific. I wanted to see Josephine one more time before I left, so I hitchhiked from Riverside to Anaheim. I spent the night with your mother . . . on the couch . . . next to her mother, Matilda.

In the morning, I hightailed it up to the base. We must have gotten word in the middle of the night that we were being shipped out because everybody was in full army dress with their backpacks on and in formation. I heard my name, "Carl Carpenter!" and hollered out "Here!" Jimmy had put all my stuff where I was supposed to be. I put on my gear, and on Easter of 1942, I got on a boat to Hawaii. That was the last time I saw your mother for four years.

> *Hup, two, three, four,*
> *hup, two, three, four,*
> *hup, two, three, four,*
> *hup . . .*

We marched up and down those beaches of Hawaii for eight months but never saw anything. That's where my knees started to break down—was the beginning of the end for that in '42. We never saw anything until they flew about thirty of us guys and a couple of lieutenants into the interior of Luzon Island in the Philippines. What a lot of people didn't know was that the Japanese had gone into the Philippines and dug trenches and learned trench warfare years before they invaded us. We had absolutely no training in that. We didn't know how to beat 'em. I mean, Reg, I trained with a *broomstick*. Our job was to draw the Japanese out of their bunkers and caves. I was a flamethrower. I carried a sixty-eight-pound tank of gasoline and napalm on my back. We'd find the Japanese burrowed up in the trenches and caves, and when the Lieutenant gave the signal, I shot the flame into the cave. That soldier caught on fire, ran out, and one of us would shoot him. It was a mercy killing, really. If they didn't come out, we starved them to death. I did that on Luzon Island from 1942 to 1945.

People ask me, "Carl, why were you a private when you went into the army and a private when you came out?" I say, "Have you ever met an officer?"

One day, we were staking out the Japanese at this place where there were two hills. The hills felt like mountains by then because we were sick from malaria and dysentery and my knees were really going about this time—I had been in and out of the barrack hospital for them, but they'd just patch me up and send me back out. Our lieutenant told us that the Japanese were at the top of the second hill. "Run up the first hill, set up, and shoot them" were our orders. It was the middle of the day and hotter than blazes. The lieutenant gives us the signal, and we start running up the hill. All of a sudden, bullets are flying at us, and a lot of the guys were killed. The lieutenant started screaming "Retreat! Retreat!"—like we needed to be told. The Japanese were at the top of the hill we were running up, picking us off one by one. "I read the map wrong," he yells, white as a sheet. What did he have to be scared of? He stood at the bottom of the hill while *we* took the bullets. I was one of the only guys in the platoon to survive that.

I dreamed about your mother all the time. I wrote her and asked her to marry me. When she said yes, I wrote my mother the news and asked her to buy Josephine an engagement ring and send it to her. Mother took the bus to Watertown and bought a gold ring with a nice square diamond and sent it to your mother. Then Mom wrote me and said, "Carl, now you hurry home because you've got a lot to look forward to." This was 1942 to '43.

It wasn't until 1945 that I got a break. Congress passed a law stating that battles had a certain amount of points. If a soldier had accumulated so many points, then he could go home. I had twice the points. So in April of 1945, I got on a ship with almost the whole division and went back to Hawaii. I was hoping to go see your mother, but that's not what happened. In Honolulu Harbor, they divided us up. The guys who lived west of the Mississippi were going to California to catch a train home. The guys who lived east of the Mississippi got on a new Navy ship. Instead of going back to California, we were going to go through the Panama Canal and up to New York City. It was a brand spanking new ship from the Coast Guard, which had just been started. It had a new crew and everything. That thing kept breaking down, and the crew didn't know how to fix it. All the luxury ships had been taken over for the war effort, so they transferred us to a beautiful French cruise ship with a mahogany bar and stained glass windows. I liked thinking about the people who traveled around the world on it and all the places they had gone. I volunteered for the best job and got it! Kitchen patrol was the best job because we got three squares a day and the other guys only got two. Plus, they had to sleep in the hole, and I got to sleep on the deck. I'm no idiot.

Our ship pulled into New York Harbor in August, and the only people to greet us were the Gray Ladies. The Gray Ladies worked for the Red Cross. They were called that because they wore gray dresses with a red cross pinned to their fronts. They were standing on the dock at the end of the pier, and when we got off the boat, they handed us little bottles of milk called "jills." The milk tasted so good. I had two jills—none of us guys had eaten anything fresh in five years. That milk went straight through me and all the other guys, and we all got sicker than dogs. I can't stand milk to this day.

Before we could go home, every soldier had to have what Mrs. Roosevelt referred to as "social conditioning." They said we had been in the jungle so long, we had to have the savage taken out of us. You know what that meant? *New Jersey*. We took the train to Fort Dix for social reconditioning, but what it really meant was we had to play a lot of cards for a couple of weeks. At the beginning of September, they put me on a train to Watertown. My brother Eddard picked me up at Armory Square where the whole thing had started and took me home to the St. Lawrence River and Clayton.

———————

It was a beautiful day when I got home. The river was bright blue, and it was warm. Mom and Pop's place looked great, and the garden was in full bloom. Everybody had come home to visit—Dot and Frank from New York City; Bernie and John from Florida; Eddard and Marguerite were already there; Rip and Violet, of course; Joe wasn't home from Midway yet. The rocking chairs were under the tree, and kids were playing around. It was like nothing there had changed at all. I knew something inside of me had changed, though. I had changed. That was a little strange for me. I remember we all had a couple of beers. I got tired, so I went upstairs to take a nap. First time I had a bed to myself without Joe. We shared a bed until we went into the service. I was excited about that.

"Carl, do you remember what you did?" Dot asked me later when I came downstairs.

"No," I told her.

"Mom went to wake you up. When she touched you, you started choking her. If she hadn't screamed, you wouldn't have stopped. You would have killed your own mother."

That scared me. I slept downstairs on the couch after that. Mom never woke me up again. I stayed home for a while because my mother said I needed the rest. Dot was always pestering me to "get a job, get a job." Finally, Mother said, "Leave him alone. He's been in a war, and he needs to have some fun."

And, man, *did* I have some fun! But then that fun wanted to get married. I said to that fun, "Look, I am going to marry a girl in California." You see, I had always intended to marry your mother. I got on the next train. Your mother was waiting for me at the train station. She was even prettier than when I first met her—her hair, her skin, and did I mention I could put my hands around her waist two times? It was her eyes, though. Were they cornflower blue or spring green? I still don't know.

As soon as I walked into the Kneip house, her mother, Matilda, said, "When are you going to get married?" This was in September.

I said, "Well, how about the end of September?"

"No, too soon," she said.

"Ok, how about October?" I asked.

"No, too soon. I have decided on November fifth."

That was that. My mother took the train out and stayed with Dorothy, your mother's sister. She wore a blue suit to the wedding. Matilda wore black.

On November 5, 1946, your mother came down the aisle on her father, Pop's, arm. She looked so beautiful. She had made her own dress out of cream-colored silk. Her hair was piled up with pearls in it. I kept looking at her eyes, wondering *cornflower blue or spring green?* I still don't know. The two of us stood before the altar at St. Boniface Catholic Church and took our vows:

"I, Carl Henry Carpenter, take thee, Josephine Agnes Kneip,
and promise to
love, comfort, honor, and keep you,
in sickness and in health,
for richer, for poorer,
for better, for worse,
in sadness and in joy,
and to cherish and continually bestow upon you my heart's
deepest devotion,
forsaking all others,
keeping myself only unto you as long as we both shall live."

We couldn't have known it then, but every single one of those words came true.

You know, people say to me, "Carl, don't you hate the war? Look what it did to you. It made you a cripple." I always say, "No, I don't hate the war." The war brought me your mother. Without your mother, I wouldn't have you kids. I'd be just another guy from Clayton, looking for fun. Have you had enough of that story, Toots? 'Cause the game's comin' on.

My daddy was in WWII,
went in at eighteen, came out at twenty-two.
Married my mama in Cal-i-for-ni-a;
both lived to rue and bless the day.

Bendable Barbie

My father sold sewing machines at Sears. Before that, he peddled the *World Book Encyclopedia* door to door.

"And for a low, low additional price, madam, may I also interest you in the children's *Childcraft* series? It is FULL of the highest quality POH-et-try, LIT-trah-chure, and muh-UUU-sic. Why, madam, it is guar-an-TEED to raise your child's IQ fifty points or fifty percent, whichever is higher," he promised.

He got fired from that and slid down the salesmen's ladder to sell Fuller brushes. He told every dirty joke about the farmer and his daughter that went with the territory.

"I can sell anything to anybody. Why, I once sold a car to a man who already owned it," he swore on a stack of Bibles.

But truth be told, my pop was really a family man, so he settled down with Singer at Sears.

"Buttonhole. Embroidery stitch. Zigzag," he demonstrated.

It was the year of the aluminum Christmas tree with the revolving colored lights.

"You know, kids, it just doesn't smell like Christmas this year," my mother sniffed as she wandered with her wintergreen spritzer.

It was the Christmas of bendable Barbie. That Christmas, the war which waged in my father's mind and played out on the domestic battlefield extended a white sheet of temporary surrender. But great wars are made up of a series of small battles marked by defeats and triumphs. We called those battles "Christmas."

ORANGES CHRISTMAS

We're living in the blue house on Mary Street. This year, Dad emphasizes the *traveling* over the *salesman*. Our mother cries, "Pray for coal in your stockings, kids. We need it for heat!"

No tree.

No presents.

Just the burning look in our mother's eye as she puts on fire engine–red lipstick.

Clutching her purse, she marches down the front steps and tramps through the snow to the fence between our house and the neighbors'. Crossing herself, she snaps a bedraggled pine bough off one of their evergreen trees. They are Catholics too. She's counting on absolution.

Shaking off the snow, she carries the bough into the kitchen and crucifies it to a square board with long nails. I am watching from a lopsided stepladder in the corner of the kitchen. Heat is blasting out of the open oven door. The bright yellow canary in its cage sings along to the birdsong record playing on the portable hi-fi.

My mother takes some walnuts and spray-paints them gold and then glues loops of thick red yarn to the top. She is quiet and concentrated as I watch her affix the golden walnuts to our paltry Christmas tree in the shapes of the constellations.

On Christmas Eve night, all five of us kids huddle on the piece of plywood that's our couch. My mother snaps off the lights and shines a flashlight onto the tree. As she rotates it, we "ooooh" and "aaaah" at Orion's Belt and the Milky Way. We even have the North Star that led the Wise Men to the baby Jesus.

My father makes his specialty: dough Johnnies. The house fills with the aroma of yeasted dough rising unevenly on the cold heating grate, and we feel full just from the smell. After punching it down three or four times, Dad fries it in an iron skillet until the crust is brown and stiff. We slather the dough Johnnies with margarine, rip into them with our teeth, sing "Joy to the World," and go to bed.

On Christmas morning, there are seven oranges under the tree. My mother has carved each of our names into the peel in her beautiful handwriting script—*David. Timothy. Cynthia. Mary. Regina.* I'm the youngest, so I am handed mine last. The orange oil covers my hands, and the small sacks of juice burst in my mouth. It tastes so sweet.

SPAGHETTI TURKEY CHRISTMAS

Turns out we were rich on Oranges Christmas compared to Spaghetti Turkey Christmas. Dad had been in the hospital so long with no back pay that Mom couldn't make two pennies squeak together. Waiting in the welfare food line at church, we hear people mumble as they walk past us, "Damn breedin' Catholics. They always have more kids than they can feed."

Why do people think that when you're poor, you're deaf?

Spaghetti Turkey Christmas begins like every other day that winter. All five of us kids stream down the stairs and stick our feet in the oven to warm up. Ten legs—fifty little wriggling toes—are stuck in our oven.

"Hey, Reg, this is just like that story," my sister Mary says to me while I sit in her lap.

"Which one?" I ask her.

"You know, *Hansel and Gretel*, where the witch tries to eat the kids by sticking them in the oven. Maybe Mom is secretly a witch," she says, sounding worried.

Mom does have a pointy nose . . . I slowly pull my feet out of the oven.

My father has been gone since the spring bullhead season. They keep doing one operation after another on him. First, they scrape the knee cartilage and then remove his kneecap. Little by little, they are cutting pieces of my father's leg out—with his permission—because he'll do anything to prevent it from being amputated. We don't have a car, and my mother can't drive anyway, so we look at his picture to remind us that he lives with us. The veteran's hospital has scheduled an ambulance to bring him home at ten o'clock on Christmas morning. At nine o'clock, guys my father grew up with knock on the front door. Milt, Rory, Sullivan, Natali, and Pete stand in a shivering clump on the porch. They've come to clean the sidewalk so my father won't fall down. Standing at the window, we watch them shovel the hard, crusty snow off the uneven walk, and then Pete pulls out a blowtorch. Crouching, he directs the straight blue flame back and forth to melt any remaining snow and ice. Finally, Mr. Natali salts the sidewalk. "Like an Eye-talian making fish," he says, and the guys laugh. My mother goes out and hugs them on her tippy toes and wishes each one a Merry Christmas. She comes inside, and we all stand at the window to wait.

At ten o'clock, the ambulance rambles down Mary Street. It's a big white truck with double back doors and blue letters on the side that spell A-M-B-U-L-A-N-C-E. The back doors open, and my father emerges. He is unsteady and thin with yellow-tinted skin. My mother gasps then runs out to meet him. His arms open wide. They embrace and kiss a long, tangled-up kiss. I watch my parents from the window like they're in a movie. He is the returning wounded warrior, and she is the lonely war bride, knocked up five times. When he enters, it's as if the lights go on by themselves. He tries to kneel but can only stoop. We are wary but welcoming. Who is this man who looks like our father? I break the ice and grab him around his waist. My siblings soon follow, and we hang on him like ornaments. It's

Christmas, and our savior has come. We got no presents. We got no tree. We don't care. The day gets even better when my mother pulls me aside.

"Regina, I am not going to make a ham or a roast beef. This Christmas, I am going to make your favorite supper—spaghetti," she whispers only to me.

Spaghetti! I beam at my mother. Can she turn water into wine, too? Mom disappears into the kitchen to prepare the feast. My father hobbles into the dining room to sharpen the knives. He grabs ahold of the sharpening stone and hocks a big glob of spit onto it, then drags the biggest carving knife we own across the stone in a motion too fast for the human eye to see. When it's razor sharp, he yanks a hair out of his head and pretends to cut it in half.

"Sup-per," my mother sings out from the kitchen.

We scramble to our seats. My father stands at his rightful place at the head of the table. All our eyes are glued to the kitchen doorway. Slowly, my mother emerges from the kitchen with a turkey platter in her hands. On the turkey platter is a turkey sculpted out of spaghetti! She winks at me and places the spaghetti turkey right in front of my father. It will go perfectly with the water. My mother sits at the opposite side of the table, and we bow our heads in prayer.

Bless us, O Lord,
and these thy gifts . . .

I steal a glance at my long-absent father. His face is pinched with pain while his eyes dart back and forth from us kids to the empty stockings to my mom. It's as if he and I are one. Moments ago, I was in a cozy and happy house, but now I see what he sees: a plywood couch, plaster missing from the walls, wooden crutches in every corner of every room, and faded family photographs behind frames of cracked glass. My mother's sewing machine is ready to put a new patch over the old patch on Dave's jeans. Our home is clean but barren and filled with broken things repaired with tape and nails. One man's trash is our household. My eyes become my own again, and the room, which felt warm a moment ago, is now chilly, as if the earth has rotated away from the sun too quickly. I look upon my father. His eyes slowly come to rest on the spaghetti turkey. He looks downcast and ashamed, like we look when we stand in line to get our food. I have just eaten from the tree of knowledge. My father is not a god but a man. I am now an outcast from the Garden of Eden. We *are* poor and Catholic. How did I not notice? I turn my eyes away and pray.

> *. . . which we are about to receive*
> *from thy bounty,*
> *through Christ, our Lord.*
> *Amen.*

Dad starts carving the turkey. I really want a drumstick. Then something happens to my father. Maybe the sunlight hit the silverware just wrong or a sound startled him or a war memory crept in. We don't know and never guess. Whatever it is that lives inside him comes out, and he is standing there as pale as skim milk, sweating and trembling. He smells like a burnt match and grows three feet in height. In a raging fit, he picks up the spaghetti turkey platter and hurls it across the dining room. His lips are pulled back and his teeth are showing. Standing at the head of table, holding the sharp carving knife in his hand, his eyes dart back and forth at us kids. He's been gone almost six months, but we all remember what that look means. My mother, the general, quickly retreats into the shadows of the kitchen. My brothers and sisters and I, fellow foot soldiers, duck into the foxhole under the table. In my father's massive hands, the plates become bombs and the silverware turns into bullets. Now we are in the Philippines on the island of Luzon with Private Carl Henry Carpenter, the flamethrower, as he crawls with a tank of fuel on his back looking for Japanese soldiers to set on fire. Twenty years ended, but here the war rages on. My sibling prisoners of war and I huddle under the table. Strewn all around us is the dissected spaghetti turkey. Picking up a strand, I twirl it around my tongue and slurp. It is my salvation. It tastes oddly sweet.

AMBUSH CHRISTMAS

We're sticking our feet in the oven when my mom snaps.

"I've got starving kids on my hands . . . When am I going to get my husband's back disability pay? . . . If you had children, you would know what I mean . . . Your mother would be ashamed of you if she knew what you were doing," she yells into the phone at the veteran's disability claim officer one day.

There must have been something in the tone of her voice to make the man hup-two because within days my mother gets a check for fifteen hundred dollars. When she opens the envelope, that fiery look in her eye flares up. A few days later, she applies fire engine–red lipstick, grabs her hat, coat, and me, and walks up to 422 James Street. Aubrey's Grocery Store stands on the corner of James Street and Mary Street with a *FOR SALE* sign in the window. Tightly clutching her purse in one hand and my hand in the other, she slaps twelve hundred dollars on the counter.

"I'll pay you cash for your store and the house, but you have to sell it to me right away," she says to an astonished Aubrey behind the counter.

"Sold," is the answer.

Jubilant, we carry our broken stuff up the street in laundry baskets, paper bags, and wagons. The cat trots back and forth with us. Cindi, Mary, and I share the back bedroom. Mary's in the top bunk, and I get the bottom. Cindi has her own twin bed. The cat plays favorites and lays a dead mouse on Cindi's pillow every morning. Dave and Tim share the front bedroom. The portable hi-fi blasts out records by The Turtles and Iron Butterfly. My parents' bedroom is in the middle.

Mom buys a sign for the store that reads *Carpenter's Grocery: cold beer, bread & milk.* A few weeks after the sign goes up, the *c* falls off *cold*, so it's *old beer, bread & milk.* That suits us and everybody else just fine. You can buy daily essentials at Carpenter's Grocery, like the newspaper, penny candy, and dented canned goods. People can pay their phone and electric bills, too, and send or receive a Western Union telegram. My mother runs the store, and when Dad gets out of the hospital, he starts selling sewing machines at Sears.

With regular money coming in, my mother starts her "Santa slush fund." She puts away five dollars a month to purchase multiple gifts for everyone, and that Christmas morning, we see the benefits of her frugality. There are lots of shining, wrapped-and-bowed presents under the tree. After Mass, we sit down to breakfast.

"The reason Monsignor can mumble a full Latin mass in under forty-five minutes, kids, is 'cause he got shot in the jaw in the Spanish-American War. That's why he drinks too much sacrificial wine, too," Dad tells us over flapjacks.

The agony of waiting is killing me. Finally, we make our way over to the tree and say our blessing excitedly.

> *Bless us, O Lord,*
> *and these thy gifts*
> *which we are about to receive*
> *from thy bounty,*
> *through Christ, our Lord.*
> *Amen.*

As soon as the blessing is over, we're off! Everybody grabs their presents and starts ripping. Amidst the frenzy, I hear crying. It's Cindi. She has only one gift. It was beige. My mother calls me over.

"Take these five dollars and go down to Kennedy's Pharmacy and

Emporium and buy your sister that perfume she likes. You know the one?" she whispers.

I nod and bundle up in my snow pants, extra socks, coat, gloves, scarf, hat, and boots and go out the front door of Carpenter's Grocery. Softly singing Christmas carols, I slide down the granite sidewalks. Sidewalks in Clayton are like a seven-year-old's teeth, all wonky and uneven. I stop in front of Kennedy's Pharmacy and Emporium. The right side of the store is an old-fashioned apothecary with rows of large, clear, colored bottles and jars filled with roots and powders. We suspect he keeps the pickled brains behind the counter. The other side of the store is an old-fashioned soda fountain with shiny chrome stools that whir when you twirl them. I press my face against the cold plate-glass windows. The lights are off. The doors are locked. In my town, you are a Catholic, a Baptist, or a Protestant. Today is Christmas. Kennedy's Pharmacy is closed. What was my mother thinking? I stare at the display in the big picture window. Three bottles of my sister's favorite perfume sit on separate rotating stands made of clear acrylic plastic. The bottles are deep twilight pink and flare out at the bottom like Cinderella's dress at the ball. The name of Cindi's perfume is written in gold script across the bottle: *Ambush*. When I come home empty handed, I will ask Cindi if she wants my doll who can grow hair when you push a button.

BENDABLE BARBIE CHRISTMAS

It is 1965 when big changes come to Clayton. We get a stop sign at the corner of James Street and Riverside Drive.

"It's the end of civility," my father declares.

My mother has replaced her hand-crank cash register with an electric one, while my father still demonstrates buttonholes at Sears. My brothers are wearing their hair below their ears.

"I'll cut it off in your sleep!" my father rants.

My sisters want to wear their school dresses above the knees.

"It's a sin!" my mother chastises.

Mary and Cindi leave home with their skirts long. When they get to the Schaeffers' house, they safety-pin the hems up above their knees and unpin them again at the end of the school day. We are also receiving telegrams with black lines across the top addressed to our neighbors whose sons are in the Vietnam War. My father's shoulders slump when he hand-delivers those, and he smokes a lot when he comes home.

But what are hemlines and hairdos to a seven-year-old? The most important change is about to take place in my beloved doll, Barbie. In 1965, Barbie's parents, Mattel, gave their baby a skeleton. Not everywhere, of course. Her midriff and genital area were still made out of molded rigid plastic, as they are today. Prior to 1965, when Barbie and her boyfriend, Ken, wanted to embrace, I had to stick their arms out in front of their bodies and lunge them toward one another.

"I love you, Barbie," Ken says in his suave, manly voice.

"I love you, Ken," Barbie whispers in a high tremolo.

To simulate kissing, I click their heads together. But in the magical year of 1965, Barbie's arms and legs become soft and pliable. They are rubbery, fleshlike, and skin covered with bendable wire bones and lifelike joints. Now Barbie can pose in all kinds of positions.

Playful—arms up, legs in an inverted *V*, hair flowing down her back.

Jaunty—one arm on hip, one leg jutting forward, hair in braids and oh so carefree.

Professional—one arm bent in toward her chest, legs together, hair contained within a tight bun.

I *really* want a bendable Barbie. I know they are being sold in major retail stores across America, like Sears, where my father is selling sewing machines. I beg my father for a bendable Barbie.

"I don't know, Toots. That's a pretty expensive doll," he says.

At seven years old, I have had enough Christmases under my belt to know I might get what I want but I could also get something beige. On Christmas Eve, I brush my teeth and go to bed in the room I share with my sisters. Mary turns into jackhammer-head in the upper bunk. She lifts her head off the pillow and slams it down over and over again until she goes unconscious or falls asleep. I lie in the lower bunk, absorbing the radiant shock, and finally fall asleep. Waking first on Christmas morning, I quickly pad down the beige vinyl carpet runner into the kitchen. The sun is still sleeping. Mom has unplugged the revolving colored lights on the aluminum Christmas tree. In the dim living room, I quickly scan all the presents for one the size and shape of a bendable Barbie. There isn't one.

"I don't care," I tell myself and turn to go back upstairs. As I turn, I see something lined up against the baseboard in the living room.

Playful.

Jaunty.

Professional.

At least twenty bendable Barbies have been posed against the baseboard. There is the vixen black-haired Barbie, the coquettish red-haired Barbie, and the socially-acceptable-but-not-very-interesting blonde Barbie. As I creep closer, I see that each Barbie has something wrong with her. There's torn skin at the knee joints, ripped-out arms, partial legs, cut elbows, and missing hair. One Barbie has metal poking out of a huge gash in her leg. Each one of the Barbies has been damaged in some way. This gift is gorgeous and grotesque. This present manages to be both beautiful and beige.

What has happened to these Barbies? What are they doing here at my house? I wonder.

Then I understand. They have been in a war—I know all about that.

I go to work. Walking into the kitchen, I get a piece of white paper and fold it in half the long, skinny way, draw a red cross on the front of it with a crayon, and bobby-pin it to my hair. Now I am in the Florence Nightingale Brigade. In the bathroom, I grab a wad of toilet paper for bandages and some ketchup from the refrigerator to make the wounds look more realistic. I get my brothers' white toy truck from the garage and write A-M-B-U-L-A-N-C-E on the side in blue marker. When my parents pad down the beige vinyl carpet runner an hour later, most of the Barbies are recovering quite nicely from their witch hazel anesthesia. The rest are waiting for their scheduled surgeries. I run to my father.

"Thank you for my Barbies. I love them!" I cry.

"Ya like 'em, Toots? I got 'em just for you. They were the rejects! Can ya believe it? Cost me a buck," he smirks.

He tosses me up into the air and catches me. My father always catches me. As he pulls me into him, my arms wrap around his shoulders. He smells like Aqua Velva and VO5 and cigarettes.

"Merry Christmas, Toots. Merry Christmas," he whispers.

Dead Man's Float

Stand on the town docks in Clayton and look out. Directly in front of you is Calumet Island. Its name is spelled out in white rocks amid the lighthouse and pine trees. Then let your eye catch the tree line of Canada in the background. Now drift your gaze to the right, and you'll see Grindstone Island just around the bend. After that, all you see is water and sky—just water and sky on the world's largest fresh-water seaway and one of the largest rivers in North America. But what I see is a river made not just of water but of ancestral blood that carried my people from Canada to Clayton in a rickety boat. I see the Calumet Island lighthouse photograph that has graced the cover of the Clayton Central School yearbook for decades now. Grindstone holds memories of swimming at Potter's Beach and the long line of poplar trees that mark the graves of the island people who died from diphtheria so long ago. To me, this is The River: magical, magnifi-cent, and immeasurable. Its seasons are reliable but unpredictable, like mothers and God and grab-bag candy.

———————————————

The plows make snow towers over ten feet high down at Mercier's

Beach. Neighborhood kids take turns throwing each other down the side just for the right to yell "I'm King of the Mountain!" from the top. Dave and Tim take turns being King and Prince. Mary and Cindi go to skating parties at the rink by the baseball field. They warm up next to potbellied stoves constantly fueled with wood by Mr. Ferguson, and Jack Frost leaves swirling ice pictures on the window of my unheated bedroom every morning. The sound of tires crunching in the snow tells us the temperature and if we should get out of bed willingly or not. Icy sidewalks and trees line the path to school. Farmers gather on the channel near McCormick's restaurant for weekend horse-and-buggy races. My mother bundles all five of us kids up, and we slide on our bellies, like penguins, to the festivities. She brings a flask of hot cocoa. My father brings a flask of something else. The plows clear the snow off the channel as farmers clean the horses' hooves and hitch them to black buggies. Rustling farmers corral horses into circles. Ice spray flies, and horse snot and spit freeze into ropes that break midair before tinkling down. These are the regular winters on the St. Lawrence River.

In the really cold winters, when it's consistently below zero, the river freezes about as thick as a man's arm is long. On those frigid winter nights, my father teaches us how to walk across the channel using the stars and a stick as our map. He is looking for some fun on Grindstone Island, where Emmet Dodge lives. On Friday nights, Emmet takes out his fiddle, plays a tune and calls out round dances and square dances until it's time to call it quits. My father loves to dance, especially to Emmet's playing, so he gets us all bundled up. Starting at Mercier's Beach, we string out like a line of fish with my father as the bobber. The sounds of snow and ice are the real thermometers in winter, not a silver line in a glass cylinder. Cold, crackling air and cracking sheets of ice tell you to go around, get off, or move forward. It's your ears, not your eyes, that save your life on a big river like ours. The cold forces us to breathe deeply through our mouths. We exhale balls of ice onto our scarves. Woolen socks warm our feet in hand-me-down, patched-up boots. We stand in a line: Dad, Dave, Tim, Cindi, Mary, and then me. With a long and thick stick, my Pop stabs the ice in front of us until he hears a *ttch* sound and says, "Yeah, it's frozen. Walk here."

Ttch, step, *ttch*, step, *ttch*, step . . .

Slowly, we make our way across the river.

Ttch, ttch, ttch. We form a snake line, holding hands and spreading out so there isn't too much weight in one place. Dad's cigarette smoke hangs in the air like fingers pointing the way. Cold nights mean clear nights and a sky full of stars. In those snot-freezing winters, Dad *ttch*es us across the white channel slab all the way to Grindstone Island. From Aunt Jane's Bay, it's a short walk up the road to the community center where we find our fun. Emmet calls out the dances and saws away on the fiddle. Everybody's out: the Meeks, the Dodges, the Gaurnseys, the Turcottes, and the Potters. We dance late, then bundle up, and Pop gets us back home.

Ttch, ttch, ttch.

———————

Most people know it's spring when the trees leaf out, the scent returns to the air, the worms begin their expedition across roads just to see what's on the other side, and birdsong floats in the windows. To us, those are arbitrary signs of spring. We know it's spring when the jalopy someone has driven, pushed, or towed to the middle of the channel falls through the ice. First day of spring!

In the fall, the river takes off the china-blue dress she wears all summer long and changes into a gray-green dress with lace and swiss voile polka dots. She takes up smoking again, mostly in the mornings. French inhales of wispy smoke curl into the air at dawn. An international woman of mystery, she stops speaking English and switches to her other language, French. All summer long, the river says, "Lap, lap, lap." But listen closely in the fall—"Glip, glip, glip," she gurgles.

Summer is best of all.

On June 24 at 3:15 p.m., the last bell of the school year rings. My sister Mary and I run home, burst through the door of Carpenter's Grocery, kick off our shoes, and yell, "Mom, we're going fishing!"

"No, you're not. You might lose an eye," she warns.

What? Her constant concern for our well-being forces us to lie to her. We don't want to commit the sin of lying, but we have to or we will *die*.

"Yes, Mother, we shall obey you," we say angelically while keeping our fingers crossed behind our backs. When she smiles approvingly and turns away, Mary and I sneak down the basement stairs and hide in the coal bin to make clandestine fishing poles. A willow stick makes a pole, string is the line, and paper clips bend into hooks. We get some balls of Wonder Bread bait and sneak down to the municipal dock where we spend the entire day reeling in one inedible fish after another. We haul in carp, baby perch, sunnies, catfish. One day, Mary catches an eel off the end of the dock in the deep water. It's flopping around, smothering in the air, and she cries out, "Don't touch it! Don't touch it! It's an electric eel. You're gonna get electri-fried!"

Mary is four years older than me, and she knows everything.

"Swallow a cherry pit, Reg; a cherry tree'll grow out your ears."

"Swallow a watermelon seed, Reg, and you're gonna poop out a watermelon. It isn't gonna be a sugar baby, either."

"Dragonflies are sent by the Pope to sew Catholic girls' legs together."

She knows *everything*.

At the end of a long fishing day, Mary and I drag our catch home. Mom sees the fish and the poles and says, "Girls, put this sin on your list for confession." Dad smiles approvingly and gets out the cutting board. Everybody in our town has a cutting board in their backyard. Pop guts, scales, and then fries the fish in his secret batter that has something to do with beer. Cindi loves the tails crunchy, like potato chips, so he burns those for her. At night, Mary and I sleep in the same bed. We drift off to sleep after talking about perch and what makes the best bait.

When we aren't fishing, Mary and I swim at Mercier's Beach. Mercier's Beach is a cove, really, with a gently sloping sandy bottom and no current. Everybody learns to swim there on Saturday mornings with Mrs. Brabant, our gym teacher.

No matter what time of year you see Mrs. Brabant, she wears the same thing: white Keds, white socks, white tennis shorts, a white tennis shirt, white lipstick, and an orange gym teacher's whistle. No matter where she is—at church, out walking, grocery shopping, at the library; it doesn't matter—she has on that whistle.

"Regina," Mrs. Brabant says in an English accent, "would you please demonstrate how to do the dead man's float properly?"

Why does she talk that way? I think. *She's from Clayton, too.*

I stand up proudly in my two-piece cobalt-blue spandex bathing suit and throw myself face first into the water. My arms splay at my side. My face goes slack while I imagine myself drifting aimlessly, awaiting a WWII U-boat to come and pick me up. I count *one one thousand, two one thousand, three one thousand, twenty-five one thousand* and pop up, gasping for air. Mrs. Brabant says, "Class, that is how you do the dead man's float *properly.*"

After swimming lessons, Mary and I hide behind the sand dunes. They are just little hills, but we call them "dunes." We hunker down and wait for girls Cindi's age to come down. These girls are mature, maybe thirteen or fourteen years old. They wear polka-dotted, molded, rigid plastic Styrofoam bikinis with power bows at the hips. They spread their blankets under the large oak tree and begin to beautify.

Globs of emerald-green Dippity-do hair sculpting gel turns hair into spiky horns. Slabs of hair are rolled onto extra-large orange juice cans that get stabbed with bobby pins the size of railroad stakes. Next, they smear their bodies with skin stain: baby oil and iodine. Everything gets pinned, slathered, and glued into place. The allure trap is set. Now all they have to do is wait for boys.

Mary and I wait too. We know something these girls don't know: the sand at Mercier's Beach is full of sand fleas. After a while of discreet itching, they lose their cool, jump up, scream like banshees, and rip their skin off. It's very attractive. We jump up too and run down to the water to have an underwater tea party.

Have you ever been on the exclusive list of an underwater tea party? In case you get an invitation, this is the proper etiquette: jump way up, cross your legs, hold your nose, and sit on the bottom with your eyes open. Then pretend to drink tea at Harrods with the Queen, pinky fully extended, while holding a scintillating conversation in fishspeak.

"Hblblelloblbl. Hblblow are youblbl?"

"Goodblbl. Howblbl are youblbl?"

"Goodblblbbbb."

Pop to the top and scream, "Did you hear what I said? I said 'Hello'!"

When we aren't fishing in the river, we're swimming in it. When we aren't swimming in it, we're wading in it. When we aren't wading in it, we're bathing in it. When we aren't bathing in it, we're peeing in it. And when we aren't peeing in it, we're drinking from it.

Growing up on the St. Lawrence River is a magical experience. The river is like a Great Mother to us. She is a great womb in which we all grow. But like all mothers, the river can be changeable and moody.

She can be a Great Mother or a Terrible One who asks one of us down to her playground to play for keeps, like with the Thompson boy.

He's my brother Tim's age, sixteen, all gangly and pimply. One late afternoon, he takes his boat out to do a beer run in Canada when a storm rolls in. His boat capsizes, and he drowns. Our house is near the docks. When the firefighters fish his boat out that night, they park it in front of a picture window that says *Salada Tea*. The red safety lights on the back of his boat are still flashing. All five of us kids and our mother stand at the window. James Street is slick and shining from the rain. The freshly painted white line down the middle is glowing. We watch Mrs. Thompson run down the middle of James Street. Her body is silhouetted by the streetlights, her hair wild, her arms flailing. She is crying, "My son, my son . . ."

We cluster together with that horrible combination of sympathy and gratitude—so sorry she has lost her son, so grateful it isn't one of us.

When the river acts up, the mothers form a brigade against her. Our mothers tell us that we aren't allowed to go down to the river unless one of them is with us. That means we will never go, because mothers don't have fun. If they look outside and can't see us in the yard or if we don't answer their call, the tin can telephones drop from the sky and the news spreads from one ear to the next. All the mothers fan out across the docks and beaches and start calling our names. A song of names rings out in the air over the waves and boats—"Mar-y! Tim-othy! Cyn-thia! Suuu-san! Regi-na!" If we don't come right away, we later have a burning backside that reminds us we should have.

Still, we listen because we are afraid.

But *not* going to the river is like not remembering how to breathe or forgetting your own name. We can't do it. We can't shun the river. The river is one of us. Slowly, one by one, we sneak back down to the river with our balls of Wonder Bread bait and our homemade fishing poles. We swim. We fish. We wade. We practice doing the dead man's float.

It's a Miracle

It's Wednesday afternoon at two o'clock and Mrs. Kinney, my fifth grade teacher, announces, "Those of you going to religious education may be excused." Two-thirds of my class stands up, gathers their things, and joins the other students going to religious education on the sidewalk outside of Clayton Central School. True to life, we divide by denomination. The Protestants go their way while the rest of us scrappy Catholic kids meander down James Street until we get to St. Mary's Catholic School and Convent where we have all attended weekly catechism class since first grade.

The Sisters of the Holy Cross have been educating the Clayton Catholic youths since 1913. They wear floor-length black habits complete with white wimples, sensible black shoes, and heavy wooden crosses on long dangling rosary bead necklaces around their necks. Those rosary necklaces sway back and forth like pendulums and threaten to take out young children's eyes as they walk down the street single file like penguins. It was the sisters' sacred duty to put the fear of God into us, and by God, they did. With their ever-ready disciplinary rulers and penetrating looks, they drilled the prayers and rituals of Catholicism into our impressionable minds.

Despite my best efforts, I learned a lot of important things about God in catechism class through the years. For example: "Mom, Sister George told us today that God is a string bean!"

This startling statement was met with a period of silence. "I think you mean God is a *Supreme Being,* dear," my mother corrects me.

In 1965, the church changes everything with the Second Vatican Council. Now the sisters can wear gray knee-length habits that show their calves and wimples that show their bangs. They can also stop taking the male names of the saints and instead take the female names. The organ is replaced with the folk guitar, and Monsignor slurs the mass in English instead of Latin while drinking the sacramental wine. The church also allows laypeople to teach us catechism. This is a huge relief because whenever the nuns tell us a Bible story, someone's eyes get gouged out.

My catechism teacher that year is also my neighbor, Mrs. Hunt. "She's a pretty good egg for a convert," comments my father.

I enter my classroom, take the desk next to the window, and start doing homework in my favorite subject—daydreaming. My studies are interrupted when Mrs. Hunt asks me to read Ezekiel 47:9 aloud:

"There will be swarms of living things where the river flows. Where the river flows, there will be many thousands of fish because the river flows there. The salt water will be made fresh because the river flows there. Where the river flows, there will be many living things."

After the reading, Mrs. Hunt tells us the story of the loaves and the fishes—when Jesus fed the multitudes by transforming a couple of fish into lots of fish and a few loaves of bread into many loaves of bread. Everyone goes home with their bellies full and filled with the spirit. She ends the lesson by telling us, "Children, never stop believing in miracles."

As Mrs. Hunt is preparing us for Jesus to rise from the dead, the river is undergoing a resurrection of its own. Another winter has come and gone, and the usual telltale signs of spring are popping up all over Clayton: the trees bud out, the scent returns to the air, and the worms make pilgrimages across the road just because they can. Ice as thick as a man's arm begins to melt, and at night, the floes crash into one another like carnival bumper cars. A juggernaut of a ship with a large drill attached to its hull grinds its way through the ice on the St. Lawrence Seaway to make way for the winter-moored freighters to move their heavy cargoes from one part of the world to another. As everyone in town is preparing for Easter, my father is preparing to practice his own religion: bullhead fishing.

On the first full moon after the spring equinox, thousands of spawning bullheads will fill the creeks and tributaries of the St. Lawrence River. Bullheads will crowd one another in the water surrounding Grindstone Island and Wellesley Island and our favorite fishing spot, French Creek Bay. The bullhead is a beautiful fish. It's got a yellow belly, a black top, whiskers like a catfish, and horns on top of its head. Carefully smooth down those horns when pulling your hook out of its mouth or the horns will poke you and fill your palm with poison. A bullhead has no scales on its skin, and in the spring, their flesh is tender and sweet. The only time of year you want to eat a bullhead is in the spring because they are bottom feeders. When spring turns to summer, the water along the shore and the bullhead's flaky, tender, sweet meat gets muddy. The bullhead is sorely in need of orthodontia. They have an unsightly underbite that allows them to scoop worms into their mouths. Bullheads don't pluck a worm off a hook just dangling in the water. They lurk in the cool shadows of the creek and wait for their food to come to them, and when it does, they open their mouths and scoop the ball of worms, concealing the hook in their mouths, and they're yours.

The full moon after the spring equinox is on a Thursday that year. Of us five kids, only my sister Mary and I want to go fishing with Dad. He tells us we're in charge of the worms. A soft rain has fallen earlier that evening, perfect for nightcrawlin'. When it's dark, Mary grabs the flashlight. I can't find my shoes. She runs out the door ahead of me and goes over to the Marshalls' backyard. They've got the best mud pit filled with the longest, plumpest, juiciest, biggest worms in the world. She's way ahead of me and over by the stink bomb tree when I stand on something hard and round.

Oh my gosh, this is the biggest worm in the world. No, no, it's not a worm. It's a snake, probably just a garter snake. Wait, it's not a garter snake. It's a rattlesnake. We don't have rattlesnakes around here, but I'm sure this is one. No, it's a cobra. Oh my gosh, what if it's not a cobra? What if it's an anaconda or a boa constrictor?

"Mary, Mary," I whisper.

She runs back, disgusted with me. "Hurry up, slowpoke."

"I'm standing on a snake. If I move even the tiniest bit, it will eat me alive," I whimper.

She points the flashlight at my toes. "You're standing on a garden hose, stupid."

We gently stretch fat, thick worms out of the earth and put them into a coffee can with wet shredded newspapers in it so they don't dry out. Once it's full, we take it home and put it by the car Dad has packed with everything else we need to go bullheading: bamboo poles, a Coleman gas lantern, a ratty pink quilt to sit on, a picnic basket with butter, bologna, and cheese sandwiches wrapped in wax paper, a jug of Kool-Aid, and a flask of something else to help my father "slake his thirst." The full moon is rising, and it's time to get in the car. Dad drives through town, turns right on Cape Road, then left onto Frontenac Springs, and another left onto Crystal Springs.

The pavement gives way to gravel. The moon is shining so brightly Dad turns off the lights. The rocks in the road sparkle and lead us to French Creek. Mary and I are laughing in the back.

"Open your mouth and close your eyes," Mary tells me.

"Nuh-uh, you're gonna spit in my mouth like you did at the drive-in movie the last time," I say.

"I am not. Now close your eyes and open your mouth. I got a surprise for ya."

"No way! You're gonna spit in my mouth!"

"No, I'm not. I got a piece of candy for ya, but I'm only gonna give it to ya if you close your eyes and open your mouth."

"You got candy?" Mary knows I'll do anything for a piece of candy.

You know, worms don't taste as bad as you might think.

Dad turns around. "Stop your yappin'; the fish will hear you." We quiet down and listen to the rocks pop under the tires. Dad turns off the engine at the top of the grassy knoll, and we gather our things quietly and click the doors shut so we can surprise the fish.

Our feet are soon soaked as we walk down the dewy grass to the creek. Dad lays out the blanket, poles, worms, picnic basket, and lantern. We sit silently looking at the moon's reflection in the black water. Off in the distance, we hear our neighbor's tires popping on the gravel as they drive in the moonlit darkness to the creek. It doesn't take long before ten or more blankets are spread alongside ours. No one says a word. The smells of Kool-Aid and whiskey mix in the air. The hiss of the Coleman lanterns, the sound of unwrapping wax paper, and the mosquito's high-pitched *zzzzz* is followed by the sound of hands slapping skin.

Then, when the moon is high above us, we hear the sound we have been waiting for: bullheads are spawning down the creek. There are so many of them that their tails flap against one another as they rush forward into the narrowing water. Everyone jumps up and grabs a pole. As soon as the ball of worms hits the water, a bullhead grabs it and is yanked to shore. It doesn't take long for our picnic basket to be full, and we are home and asleep in our beds by one o'clock.

The next day in school, Mary and I are so tired we rub our eyes, but we know we have so much to look forward to that night. There's an all-you-can-eat Friday night fish fry dinner at the fireman's hall. It costs five bucks a head, and kids under twelve get in free. Plates piled with bullhead are waiting for us. As soon as we finish one, we raise our hand and a fireman brings us another. The only other food on the table is a loaf of bread. Mrs. Hunt is sitting at our table. I yell to her, "Mrs. Hunt, this is just like the story of the loaves and the fishes!" She hollers back, "Regina, life is a miracle!"

Flames of Jesus

We're living on her street—*Mary* Street—so she wins the fight and gets to fill Dad's lighter. It's the silver Zippo with the initials *CHC* scratched onto the bottom. Slowly and methodically, she intones Dad's instructions.

"Unscrew the bottom. Pack down the white cotton filter. Squeeze Zippo lighter fluid until it brims to the top. Put it all back together." She concentrates so hard her tongue flicks out her mouth.

I'm in the living room lying on my belly and coloring in the Catholic saints coloring book I got for Easter. My 64-pack Crayola crayon box with the sharpener in the back sparkles.

I color Saint Sebastian's arrow-pierced body razzmatazz red and apply a heavy layer of burnt sienna to Joan of Arc. Saint Francis is holding a bluebird and a cardinal. Jesus's soulful chocolate eyes look at the blue flame of the Holy Spirit as it pierces his dripping red heart. I'm dabbing bittersweet pink and unmellow yellow to flowers on the Our Lady of Lourdes floating Mother Mary apparition when my sister Mary appears in the archway between the kitchen and the dining room. Yellow sunlight streams through the streaked wavy-glass windows. The caged canary trills, and outside, the green bushes shimmy in the wind.

Mary is all smiles. Holding the lighter in her hand, she flips the lid, scrapes the wheel, and sparks the flint. *Whump!* The flame leaps up, straight as a nail and celestial blue. She laughs, and I do too. Then the fire sniffs the air. Like quicksilver, the flame bends down and runs up my sister's hands. She spilled lighter fluid on her skin, and now her hands are on fire. The lighter falls from her grasp and dies on the floor. Mary's hands turn a beautiful china-blue color. They are cupped like a bowl, or a holy chalice, holding the corn-flower-blue flames of Jesus. Sister Mary's mouth opens wide, but no sound comes out.

There is no sound coming from anything. There is only the color of my sister Mary's hands as she caresses the flames of Jesus. The flames flick higher and higher. She pushes them away from her body, and I witness a miracle just like Saint Bernadette at the grotto of Lourdes. Saint Bernadette held her hand over a flame and wasn't harmed.

My sister Mary lifts off the floor and hovers through the power of the Holy Spirit in the archway between the kitchen and the dining room. Her hands are full of fire. Her mouth is open, reciting a silent prayer. Her hands turn cerulean, twilight, burnt orange, and resurrection red. Then there is a fall from grace through the father, as usual.

Dad sees Mary's hands and cries out, "Jesus!" He smothers them with a dish towel. Mary falls from grace and crumples to the floor. The flames of Jesus are gone. Our father has extinguished the light of the world. Now there is a lot of sound. The canary is shrill, and the wind gusts and rattles the windows. Mary screams in agony. Her hands are pus yellow. My father hovers over her and whispers, "Jesus, Jesus, Jesus, Jesus."

The Piano

I'm a *Carpenter kid.*

I'm *one of Carl and Jo's kids.*

Our neighbors whisper behind cupped hands, "You remember Carl and Jo, don't cha? They lived over by James Street, had that little grocery store."

"Carpenter's Grocery?"

"Umm-hmm, that's the one, corner of James and Mary."

"Had the sign that read *cold beer, bread & milk* but the *c* fell off of *cold* so it was just *old beer, bread & milk*?"

"Exactly. That says it all, if you ask me."

"Me too. They met during the war. That Josephine came all the way across the country to the St. Lawrence River and never learned to swim!"

"No wonder, she had five kids."

"Six, if ya count Carl."

"It wasn't really Carl's fault that he got shot in the war, but maybe it was his fault he chased women and couldn't keep a job, but you didn't hear it from me."

"Well, what do you expect? He's a Carpenter kid. He was one of

Ben and Aggie's kids. You remember Ben and Aggie, don't cha?"

"Lived over on Union Street, by the shipyard?"

"That's the one. Didn't Aggie's house burn down?"

"With her in it. I can't stand to think of her dead, charred body lying at the bottom of the stairs."

"They say Mrs. LaLonde—the AT&T lady, you know, worked the telephone switchboard. Remember her?"

"Curled her hair up over her ears to look like telephone receivers?"

"That's the one. Anyway, Mrs. LaLonde picked up the call at the switchboard and heard Aggie say 'fire' before she collapsed. Then Gordon Cerow, he was the mayor then, told the firemen to keep the hydrants on full, but it didn't help. Too little, too late. The newspaper said it was the flue of the chimney, but . . . in late June?"

"I know what you're sayin'. Aggie smoked in bed, and she did like her beer. Puttin' two and two together, you didn't hear it from me."

"Ben, Aggie's husband, was kinda funny. What could possibly make a man try to bash his wife's brains in with a hammer?"

"No wonder they put him in the nuthouse in Ogdensburg."

"Well, whaddya expect? He was one of them Carpenter kids."

"Face it, there's just something funny about them Carpenter kids."

In my hometown, you're never who you *are*, you're only who you *come from*. Ancestral fingerprints identify you long before your name or smile. It's been said that the Carpenter family tree has roots traced back to the Prince of Darkness. People swear that Carpenter kids shake hands with Lucifer on their way out of the birth canal. The devil does everything he can to help us fulfill our destinies by putting temptation in our paths at every turn.

I am sad to say that we shamefully succumbed to the ways of sin and degradation. Before casting the first stone, however, who among us could resist *these* temptations?

Midnight buoy-hopping on a stolen flat-bottom boat in the middle of the channel on the St. Lawrence River.

Boathouses full of boats with keys in them and a river full of freighters daring you to play chicken.

A coal dock left idle after the freighters turned to oil for fuel. The dock had a ladder over a hundred feet high with a platform on top sticking out over the river. We *had* to climb the ladder, stand on the platform, and jump into the St. Lawrence River. We had to! Why? The devil told us to do it.

We fought temptation—we really did—by reenacting some forgotten Bible scenes down at the town docks.

Between each commercial building is an alley wide enough to ride a bike down. Starting at the sidewalk, one of us perches on a borrowed bike, points it down toward the river, then hops on the seat and starts pedaling hard. The wheels are shining. The playing cards clothespinned to the spokes go *flllll*. The little bell sings *Ding, ding, ding. Ding, ding.* The wheels go so fast they become a shiny blur, rolling off the dock and over the top of the water. For one shining moment of suspended animation, bike and rider hover over the water's surface. The Carpenter kids on the dock bow their heads, hold hands, and sing "Jesus rides a bike!" and "Amen." The river opens up and swallows rider and bike in one gulp. Then we haul the sunken borrowed bike out of the water and do it again, being good Catholic kids.

The flat roof buildings along the docks are tall and anorexic. The walls are a poor man's sandwich: bread with no filling. We shimmy up the rain gutter of Hungerford's Hardware and hopscotch across the roofs of the bank, Millie's clothing store, the Veterans of Foreign Wars building, Les Corbin's photography shop, the barbershop, and the Emporium until we stand on top of the premier sightseeing tour boat company of the Thousand Island region, the American Boat Tour Line. My father is gainfully employed during the summer as a tour boat operator. The Adonis tour boat is a double-decker boat and carries over two hundred sightseers. Once we're on that roof, we flatten ourselves and hang our heads over the gutter so we can look straight down.

We're smiling and twitching as tourists walk up the gangplank to find a good spot to see some islands and get sunburns. When the boat is full, my pop starts the massive engines. Water begins to bubble and roil. Will Neptune emerge with his seaweed beard, his hair made of eels, and his trident in hand? We hope so.

The boat pulls away from the dock, leaving a swirling current in its wake. Us Carpenter kids look at one another and count, "One, two, three, jump!" We drop like pencils into the swirling current, barely far enough from the propellers to avoid being chopped to bits. Sinking beneath the water, with one arm extended, we cry, "Help! Help! We're drowning!" Gasp. Sputter. Cough. Cough.

The tourists run to the back of the boat. The front of the boat lifts up out of the water as they scream, "Help! Someone save these children! They're drowning! Someone throw them a rope! Help! Help!"

My father comes over the loudspeaker. "No need to worry, folks; just some of the neighborhood kids having some fun . . . kids, make sure you're home for dinner!"

The boat evens out as they go into the channel near Calumet Island. My father announces, "Now, folks, if you look over the left side of the boat, you'll see the line dividing two great nations, America and Canada."

The tourists run to the left side of the boat. Again, the boat lifts up out of the water. Scanning and squinting at the water's surface, they say, "Where? Do you see a line? I don't see one. Did he say the left side of the boat? I don't see a line dividing America and Canada."

Dad illuminates them. "Just kidding, folks; there is no line. Now, folks, if you look directly ahead of you, you'll see Calumet Island and its beautiful lighthouse, and right after that, Millionaire's Way."

The opportunities nature gives us to exercise stupidity are surpassed only by the ones afforded us by our fellow citizens.

A very nice young man teaches seventh grade global studies across the hallway from his mother, who is our eighth grade English teacher. Patient as leopards and with stealth like lions, we wait until he is alone in his room. We circle him like a pack of wolves until he yelps and cries, "Mommy!" Hearing her cub, his mother slams her book shut mid-lesson, throws open her door, and storms across the hallway. She's so angry her garters pop open. With one mighty yank, she tears his door off the hinges, and looking straight at us, she screams, "You leave my son alone, you, you, you Carpenter . . . vermin!"

We are those Carpenter kids—too noisy, too rowdy, too defiant, too rude, too snotty, too in your face, too mouthy. Just too, too, too, too, too.

So when I want to take piano lessons at nine years old, it is something of a shock.

"What piano?" my dad queries.

"What? Piano?" My mother quivers at just the thought of a little cultural refinement in her household.

Music lessons cost $3.50 with Sister George at St. Mary's Convent. When my father hears how much they cost, he scoffs, "Oh, for God's sake, that's ridiculously expensive! She won't stick with it, and, Josephine, in case you haven't noticed, we don't have a piano."

The Lord works in mysterious ways; mothers do not.

My mother asks each one of my brothers and sisters if they will give up fifty cents of their allowance so I can take piano lessons. They say yes—Carpenter kids stick together. Then she raids her grocery money and gets the other buck fifty. For the next three years, every day after school, I come home, change into my play clothes, and then go to St. Mary's Convent to practice the piano.

When I first lift the lid of the piano at St. Mary's Convent, the devil and the Lord fight for my soul.

It is at the piano that I first go to the circus, watching the suspended thirds fearlessly release and land safely on the sixths. It is at the piano I first go skiing in Aspen while doing my arpeggios. It is at the piano I learn that the most diminished of us can become whole by moving a half step to the octave.

I always start conservatively with my scales, both major and minor. From a young age, I knew sweetness and sadness were best friends. Now I move onto simple Bach and Beethoven and always end with *daaahh, deeee, daahh, da deeee. Daaah, da deeee da daaahh*—Dvorak's "New World Symphony"—it's so hopeful.

The Lord works in mysterious ways; mothers do not.

I come home from school one day and see a 5x7x3–foot rectangle in the kitchen covered with a pink, ratty old quilt.

"What's under the quilt, Mom?"

"Don't tell your father!"

Conspiracy!

"Ohhh, Mom, what's under the quilt?"

"Regina, when your father gets home, it's *imperative* that you do *exactly* what I tell you to do. Do you understand?" She stands wringing her hands on a wet dishcloth.

"Ok, Mom. I pinky-swear."

She tiptoes over to the quilt and twirls her fingers into it. Like a magician twirling the silks covering his prized pigeons, she lifts and tosses the quilt aside and reveals an altar in the shape of a shining, black-lacquered console piano.

The Lord works in mysterious ways; mothers do not.

Weeks before, my mother put a *BE BACK AT 3 P.M.* sign on Carpenter's Grocery after my father went to work. She caught a Greyhound bus to Watertown, the nearest city. (At forty years of age, my mother still can't drive.) Once in Watertown, she walked to the piano store and chose this piano, arranged for its delivery, and agreed to pay five dollars a month for twelve years.

The Lord works in mysterious ways; mothers do not.

"Now, Regina, it is imperative that you do everything I tell you to do when your father gets home. Do you understand?"

"I do." Never before has my mother done something directly against my father without his permission. "Let me help you with the quilt."

My father comes home at 5:30 that night, as usual. After putting down his briefcase full of playing cards and chewing gum, he says, "What's under the quilt, Josephine?"

"Carl! Honey! What a surprise! Can I get you a beer?"

"Sure. What's under the quilt, Josephine?"

"Carl, did you know you have a talented daughter?"

"Uh-hunh. What's under the quilt, Jo?"

"She's the best of all the kids who take lessons."

"What's under the quilt, Josephine?"

"Carl, I don't want you worrying about the money. I've arranged to pay only five dollars a month for twelve years." Her voice fades out when she gets to the "twelve years" part.

"What is under that quilt, Josephine?" His hands like talons, he rips the quilt off the piano and then bellows, "It's going back in the morning!" My eyes fill with tears. My mother shushes me and tells me to sit down before the food gets cold.

Mom has made all my father's favorite foods for dinner and serves extra-large portions. Neither my mother nor I say a word during dinner. My father makes grunting and lip-smacking sounds. When my mother serves up warm apple pie with fresh cream for dessert, she says, "Regina, why don't you play a little something for your father before the piano goes back tomorrow?"

The Lord works in mysterious ways; mothers do not.

I sit down at my altar and say hello to the devil and the Lord. Then I go skiing in Aspen. I go to the circus, watching the trapeze artists jump from their suspended thirds to their sixths. I am reminded that the most diminished of us can become whole when moving ever so slightly over to the octave. I pay my respects to Mr. Bach, Mr. Beethoven, Mr. Chopin, and *dah, dee, dah, dah dee. Dah, dah dee, dah dee*—hopeful.

All the love, desire, and wonder a girl can feel pours out of me and into the piano for the entire evening.

The television never comes on. The radio stays off. My mother knits. My father hides his face behind the paper. At ten o'clock, I close the piano lid, say goodbye, and go to bed.

The Lord works in mysterious ways; mothers do not.

Whatever my mother did between the hours of ten that night and seven the next morning worked. I keep the piano, and on it, all the love and sweetness that can exist between a daughter and her mother plays out.

I'm a Carpenter kid.

Snap!

My eighth grade social studies teacher announced to my class one afternoon, "Kids, did you know that surveys are showing one in four adults will suffer a nervous breakdown?" His eyes then scanned the room and locked onto mine.

Oh no! I thought. *It's inevitable! Well, with odds like those and the way things have been going, I better get mine out of the way early.*

Over the next three years, a mountain of misfortune met a mudslide of bad judgment, and in the eleventh grade, something inside of me just snapped.

> *Boom, boom, ain't it great to be crazy?*
> *Boom, boom, ain't it great to be crazy?*
> *Giddy and foolish the whole day through;*
> *boom, boom, ain't it great to be crazy?*

When I am five, my sister Mary is nine. We are practicing walking on the crutches Dad used when he came home from the hospital.

The Syracuse Veteran's Hospital is a red brick building that stands erect against a sometimes-blue sky. The inside is very clean and smells like a cedar chest. My mother maneuvers us five kids through the labyrinth of veterans in wheelchairs. Some have gauzy leg stumps, and others have empty pajama sleeves safety-pinned to their chests. They all smoke a lot and ask, "Hold the elevator door, would ya?" We ride the elevator up to the fifth ward where the beds are laid out barracks-style. Their white sheets make them look like albino dominoes. Dad's always in bed, playing cards or twisting red crepe paper into poppies that veterans will sell for a nickel on Memorial Day. His leg is in a cast and elevated in a sling. It looks like a jet plane just taking off.

They've been doing a series of operations on him. First they remove his splintered kneecap, then the cartilage, and then the knee joint. Now they are fusing the shinbone and the femur bone into one long, unbendable leg bone. The ends of the raw bones are grafted together when they turn a large screw in his leg every afternoon.

"It's an experiment, Mr. Carpenter," they tell him cheerfully.

When he sees us, he's all smiles and gives us the Carpenter wave: his pointer finger comes up, swishes over, and then down. His arms open wide like parentheses. He tucks those paper poppies into my naturally curly hair. His skin is gray. I love him.

Once he's home, he can't work for long periods of time, so he smokes and plays cards in the corner. Sometimes he calls me over: "Hey, Toots, c'mere." He shoves his pinky finger into the hole the screw left in his leg. When he pulls it out, it goes *POP!*

"Magic trick," he winks.

Mary and I practice walking on the crutches. Ramming them into our armpits, we lift hydraulically up into the air. Our legs dangle and swing, then drop to the floor. We thump the rubber tips down, then lift and swing across the dining room.

Thump, swing! "I am a Tyrannosaurus rex coming to eat you!"

Thump, swing! "I'm a monkey in a banana tree!"

Thump, swing! "I'm an acrobat at the circus!"

Thump! Mary stops, eyes wide, and says, "Reg, let's learn how to go down the stairs on the crutches!" Whoo!

We run over, dragging the crutches behind us. They whack the steps and sound like playing cards clothespinned to a bike spoke. At the top, we survey the scene.

Long, narrow staircase. Open banister. Green plaster wall at the bottom. Mary says uncharacteristically, "You first."

"OK!" Smile. *Thump, swing!* I catapult through the air. The crutches clatter down the stairs. I gasp and reach for the banister. Mary gasps and reaches for me. The green wall is coming closer and closer.

Thump!

I awake on the couch. My father's massive hand caresses my forehead while the other hand tenderly pats my forearm.

"Whoo!" he says. "I was afraid I almost lost ya there, Toots. That's alright. You snapped outta it. You snapped right on outta it, didn't ya?" Wink.

I am nine when the pain and the war memories make my father smell like a burnt match sometimes. One night, he turns the color of skim milk and rips out a wall beam with his bare hands. That Christmas, Santa forgets to come down our chimney and turkeys are sculpted from spaghetti. My mother's high, sweet, tinkling laugh begins to quiet around this time.

I snap awake in Mrs. Kinney's fifth grade arithmetic class. I scored one hundred on last night's homework, and the little girl who was nice enough to do it has handwriting that looks just like mine.

I am twelve. My father can't really help himself anymore. His arms lift up and crash down upon all five of us kids like waves against a dock. He has become a monster—but I am the slayer. I jump on his back, ready to strike. He plucks me off and dashes me against the wall. I run down like a smashed egg. My mother, the general, retreats into her foxhole in her bedroom for the entire battle.

I snap awake to the school morning announcements. Dr. Forbes, our principal, is telling everyone I won the school-wide poetry contest. Later at my locker, I ask my best friend, "Amy, did you see me write a poem?" Smile.

I am fourteen when the VA does the same operation on my dad's other leg "'cause it's goin' on him."

"It's an experiment, Mr. Carpenter," they tell him cheerfully.

He is convalescing in a full-body cast in a hospital bed in our kitchen. All my brothers and sisters are gone. My mother closes our family grocery store and takes a job outside of the house for the first time. She is very unhappy. I walk home from school at lunchtime to check on my father. If his eyes are closed, I tiptoe over to the bed and put my finger underneath his nostrils to make sure he is still breathing.

My mother is absent without leaving. I know she still lives with us because I see her lipstick-stained coffee cup on the countertop. Her Scrabble game is out. She plays against herself and wins (my mother is very good at word games). Her book of Shakespeare sonnets is open. She loves Shakespeare.

I snap awake in the school auditorium. It's so hot in here I feel like a cinnamon roll in an oven. My entire town is here. The bleachers and chairs are filled. We're all listening to a high, clear, beautiful soprano voice. The voice is dipping and swooping and swirling around the room. It flies over our heads and drapes itself on our shoulders like a ribbon on a Christmas tree. Then I notice I am standing in front of my junior choir. I am singing a Christmas solo in our concert. The voice we're listening to is my voice. I have the voice of an angel. When I am done, the applause is loud and very long.

I'm sixteen. Everything has gone horribly, horribly wrong. I snap awake in the high school cafeteria. How did I get here? There's a food fight going on. Milk spurts out of a kid's nose. I turn to the kid next to me. "Hey, Ricky, what day is it?"

Direct rice-pudding hit to Judy Williams's crotch. She's wearing fish-net stockings.

"Thursday."

Mashed potatoes on Mr. Rhinebeck's back. Somebody's gonna pay.

"Have I been in school all week?"

"Sure," he responds.

J-E-L-L-O.

"What month is it?" I ask casually.

Goulash. Goulash. I love goulash. Did I eat the goulash?

"The one that starts with *nnnn*. Whatsa matter with you? You never miss. I mean, you are the class vice president."

Really? Huh.

"How am I doing?"

"Fantastic! I'm never gonna forget when you lobbied for that extra study hall and GOT IT!"

Snap. I wake up in a dark closet.

Snap. I am in the bathroom holding a vial of pills. Diuretics. Apparently, I am going to pee myself to death.

Snap. I am at the side of the road, waiting for a car to go by so I can just jump in front of it.

Snap, snap, snap, snap, snap!

My mother signs me into Southwood, the adolescent unit for disturbed and troubled teens at the St. Lawrence Psychiatric Hospital in Ogdensburg, New York.

My parents are driving me there in the red rusted Bonneville station wagon with the wood paneling duct-taped to the side. My mother is sitting in the backseat wearing fire engine–red lipstick and a blue hat. My father drives the car using his new hand controls. His matchstick legs are tucked under the dash. We're following along

Route 12 and the St. Lawrence River, which is frozen now and corpse blue. The cracks in the ice look like veins to me. The heater blasts hot air in my face. My father reaches over and tenderly pats my forearm. "Whoo! I was afraid I almost lost ya there, Toots. That's alright; you'll snap outta this. You'll snap out of it." Wink.

We turn off Route 12 and onto the winding, snowy road that leads us to Southwood. The endless expanse of lawn separating the hospital and the highway is a block of white, frozen lard, shining and sharp. Southwood looks like an enchanted castle with red, curving stone, tall turrets, and a steep slate roof. Wide, curving steps take us up onto a pillared porch. The wavy glass windows are covered with bars. The door clicks gently behind us. They are expecting me.

A pudgy attendant whisks me away and up the spiral staircase. I look down at my parents. Mom's face is clenched, but tears are running down her cheeks. Dad holds his hat in his hand. He gives me the Carpenter wave: index finger up, swish, down.

Then I'm in.

Pudgy walks me down a long, thin corridor with a series of rooms: a doctor's office, a dentist's office, an electric shock therapy room, a padded cell with a straitjacket hanging on the doorknob, and then the fifth room. The fifth room is a plain, unadorned room with two uncomfortable chairs in it. This is the room where I will meet my salvation: a tall, red-haired, red-bearded, freckled man with calm hands and big feet.

"Hi. I'm your therapist, Jim Flounders. Flounders, like the fish."

Pudgy takes me to the room directly opposite this one. The beds are laid out barracks-style, and the white sheets make them look like albino dominoes. The walls are painted mint green, and the doors are Chinese red. This is the "suicide watch" room. The paint job makes me want to. Pudgy tells me to sit me down—she's gonna read me the rules.

"Take off your clothes. You have to wear these green pajamas, this green robe, and these green slippers. You'll get your clothes back when we think you are good. Do you understand?"

I nod.

"You're not allowed to leave this room for any reason. If there *is* some reason you have to leave this room, however, knock on the wall and somebody'll come over to check on you. Do you understand?"

I nod.

"If you have to go to the bathroom, knock on the wall and someone'll accompany you, but you're going to be observed the entire time. Do you understand?"

I nod.

"You are allowed to take a shower every day. Five minutes long. You will be observed the entire time. Do you understand?"

I nod. She leaves. Another attendant comes in. I know right away she's a conflicted bird lover. Her hair is all teased up to look like a nest, but she's wearing cat glasses. She taps her pencil on her clipboard and says, "Hello. My name is Mrs. Woodcock."

"Oh," I giggle, "sorry about your name!"

Who knows why girls go crazy? When that one girl did, some people said it was because of the mother's cold heart. Others whispered it was the father's illness. The girl knew it had more to do with her own inability to tell the difference between what's visible but not real and what's invisible but completely real. Who knows why girls go crazy, but *she* went, and "sweet sixteen" wasn't all it was cracked up to be.

When the insurance and money runs out, she is thrown into the enchanted tower with the other impoverished and forsaken princesses. One night, when the wind blows and coyotes howl, the princess's molecules are moving so quickly that she actually is in two places at one time. The attendant tackles her, holds her down, thrusts himself against her, straps her into a straitjacket, and throws her onto a metal bed frame. He ties her down with ropes and bungee cords and then covers her body with a thick canvas sheet. It has a hole in it just large enough for her head. He leaves her in there until she cries out "water, water" and wets herself.

The princess awakens in a bright room with sulfurous yellow mist sifting through the air and mucus-like sunshine blasting through the barred windows. She's in the secret room in the enchanted tower where the thirteenth fairy lives. Remember the thirteenth fairy? She's the one who didn't get invited to the christening and is holding a grudge. She's arranged for the princess to get pricked on her sixteenth birthday. The thirteenth fairy has traded in her wand and gown and crown for a nurse's uniform and a hypodermic needle.

The queen sits ramrod straight next to the princess, staring off into the distance. The princess knows she's in trouble. She knows the queen knows it, too. Time for some strategy.

"Your Majesty," pleads the princess, "if you release me from these bonds, I will be your eternally faithful servant."

The queen stares off into the distance, as if she's frozen. Something has happened to the queen.

"Your Majesty, if you release me from these chains, I will sing your praises forevermore."

The queen just gazes off into the distance, as if she's frozen. What could have happened to the queen?

The princess decides to change tactics and appeal to the sovereign's maternal side. This is a risk. The queen hasn't shown it in a while, and the princess isn't sure she has one anymore.

"Mom, can you let me out of here? Please, Mom? I'll be good. I'll do anything you say. I'll do anything you want me to. Please let me out of here. Please." To the princess's surprise, she is quite sincere.

But the queen just keeps staring off into the distance, as if she's frozen. Poor queen.

Suddenly, the thirteenth fairy is there, tapping the queen on her shoulder. "Your Majesty, Your Majesty, time for you to go. We know what's best for her."

To the princess's horror, the queen stands and starts moving in right angles through the room toward the door. The princess sees her last chance walking away. She wants to shout but can only whisper, "Mom! Mom! Don't leave me here! Please."

The door clicks softly behind the queen.

Who knows why girls go crazy, but *she* went, and "sweet sixteen" really wasn't all it was cracked up to be.

I have to go to school. There are teachers for English, math, social studies, and history in Southwood. I try going to math, but the numbers blur on the blackboard. When the teacher moves his arm, it sounds like an owl's wings beating in the night.

"Just go to art class, Regi. Just go to art class," says Like The Fish.

I love art class. The room smells like turpentine and pastels. The teacher doesn't talk to me. I like that. The first day, I sit down at a heavily lacquered wooden table. Art Teacher places a Chinese calligraphy set in front of me. She tears off a long piece of white paper and places it horizontally on the table. Then, walking behind me, she picks up my hand, and together we grab the ink block and reconstitute it in the water well. Once we have enough ink, we put the block down and pick up a long bamboo brush. Together we dip the brush into the ink, flick it to a point, and then draw a long black horizontal line on the white paper. Once she sees I know what to do, she drops my hand and walks away.

I dip, flick, and make a line. Dip, flick, line. I dip, flick, line all day long. Near the end of the day, my hand surprises me and makes a vertical line that connects to the horizontal one and then a diagonal line connecting the two and a squiggly line underneath.

"What is that?" Art Teacher asks.

"It's a boat," I say.

Art Teacher walks away and says under her breath—quietly, but loud enough for me to hear it—"Oh, Lord, the sea is so great, and my boat is so small."

———————

For fun, I go to family therapy with my parents. They sit across from one another, and Like The Fish and I sit across from one another.

Mother: "I hate you."

Father: "I hate you."

Mother: "It's your fault she's in here."

Father: "It's your fault she's in here."

Me: "I hate you—no, I love you. Get away from me—no, don't leave me here!"

Something wells up within my mother. She stands up, points her finger in my face, and says, "You know whose fault it is that you're in here? It's *your* fault, and I am never signing you out."

That night, I run away.

The attendants forget to lock the downstairs bathroom window after Lori's embarrassing bout with the tummy trots. It's the only window in the entire asylum without bars, so I plan my escape after the eleven o'clock bed check. Steal clothes. Tiptoe past distracted attendant. Sneak down staircase. Wriggle out narrow opening. Drop softly into snowbank below. It's northern New York in February, so of course it's a whiteout blizzard and freezing cold. I've got no coat, no boots, no hat, no mittens, no nothin'. I've got a thin cotton sweater and canvas sneakers. I don't care.

I'm out! I'm out! They're never gonna find me!

I do a 007 rollover, spring to my feet, and run like a deer across the huge expanse of lawn that separates the highway and the hospital. The snow falls like pebbles off a bridge. My footprints fill as soon as I leave them. I'm the invisible girl! It will be hours before they know I'm gone. I get to Route 12 and run alongside the super-size snowplows. Their blades spark and squeal as they scrape the street. I'm running in the lane of light given off by the industrial streetlamps. I run and stumble and get up and run and stumble and get up and stumble and . . .

Get up, Regi! Get up! Get up! Run! Run! Run!

I run two miles, four miles, then five miles away from the hospital.

I'm out. I'm out. They're never gonna find me! They're never gonna find me!

There's a one-lane road off the highway. Turning onto it, I pant, pant, pant, pant. Breath scrapes against my lungs.

I'm out! I'm out! They're never gonna find me!

The one-lane road is quiet and peaceful. The snow rolls like marbles inside of a bag. The industrial streetlamps have been replaced with Victorian-style lampposts that cast pools of shadow and light, shadow and light, shadow and light, all the way down the lane. On the right stands a grove of evergreen trees. Their branches are laden with snow and ice, and yet their boughs are lifted to the celestial heavens.

My hair is frozen to my head. My eyelashes have clumps of ice on them. My sweater is frozen stiff against my chest. My fingers are blue. I know I have feet, but I can't feel them anymore.

The wind picks up—*whoooahhhhh*—and the trees begin twirling like whirling dervishes.

The wind wraps around me like a cobra and whispers in my ear, "Oh, poor you. Why don't you lie down over there? Go ahead, lie down. There's a soft clearing under the evergreen trees."

The wind shifts and brings another voice in my other ear. "What the hell are you talking about? Don't you remember that snowmobile safety course we took? The one over in the municipal building where the instructor specifically said, 'Do not lie down in the snow. It is a sure sign of hypothermia. You are freezing to death! Don't lie down, and don't drink whiskey!'"

The trees keep twirling like whirling dervishes. And the voices keep saying, "Lie down, don't lie down, lie down, don't lie down. Lie down, lie down!"

The wind dies away. The snow stops dropping like nails from the sky. The trees stand now like sentinels. The snow starts falling gently to the ground in fat, fluffy flakes. It's twinkling and twirling like a fairy's dress at a ball. I catch the flakes on the tip of my tongue.

I snap awake. My fingers are white with cold, and my eyelids begin to droop. Where are my feet?

I look around me and realize that I'm out and they're *never* gonna find me. I'm the invisible girl.

Don't lie down, Regi. Don't lie down.

I blow on my hands and stomp my feet to warm up.

Looking down the one-lane road, I see an old, sagging farmhouse. Breaking trail, I stumble to it and climb the uneven steps. For some reason, the summer-yellow bug light is on. I knock softly, and an old woman answers. Clutching her nightgown to her chest, she tucks strands of white hair behind her ear.

"May I help you, dear?" she asks.

"Yes. I am very cold, very cold. I've run away from the mental hospital. May I use your phone to call the police? I need to call someone to come and get me. If I don't go back, I'll never get out."

The next day in the art room, I make boat after boat after boat after boat after boat. I make hundreds of boats. Near the end of the day, my hand surprises me and puts a person in the boat. Art Teacher comes over, looks at it. Dip. Flick. My hand puts another slightly larger person in the boat. Art Teacher turns to me and gently holds my face in her hands. She says to me so tenderly, "Oh, Lord, the sea is so great, and our boat is so small."

Snap.

_____

Southwood isn't my own private Shangri-La. There are other teen-agers here, boys and girls all between the ages of thirteen and eigh-teen. We have our own wards separated by a long hallway where no fraternizing is allowed. We aren't allowed to go outside, and there is no gym class, so after school is over, we usually hang out in our day rooms listening to the transistor radio or playing records on the portable hi-fi. This fairly Dickensian existence is interrupted one day when the attendants, who watch over us 24/7, announce they are going to throw us a prom. "You'll have a ball!" they say.

Big Debbie, the schizophrenic, is put in charge of decorations. We make tissue-paper flowers the size of meteors in the art room and tape them across the front of the auditorium stage where a local rock-and-roll high school band is going to play all the hits of the 1960s and early 1970s. We tape so much twisted crepe paper to the ceiling of the auditorium that it resembles a tarantula's lair. A disco ball dangles in the center of the room, and the pièce de résistance is a sparkly banner stapled to the back of the stage wall that reads *A Night to Remember*.

"You'll have a ball!" they say.

On the day of the dance, our therapist decides we need an extra group therapy session. Group therapy usually happens after meds are distributed, so conversation is often a little slow. We sit in a circle in our day room. The therapist asks, "So does anybody have anything they're hoping for tonight? Any expectations? Wishes?"

Little Laurie, no bigger than a minute, just smiles. Carol claps her hands and cries, "Boys! Boys! Boys!"

Big Debbie, who is the size and shape of a refrigerator (and just as communicative), says, "Ho Hos and Twinkies."

Val, who has a penchant for putting her fist through the window, says, "Nobody touches me!"

Shelley laughs scornfully. "Proms are stupid." She has been around the block more than once. Sandy is too busy talking to her hallucination to answer the question. Then he gets to me.

"How about you, Regi? Do you have any wishes for tonight?" asks Therapy Man. I look at the floor. *I wish. I wish.* "Everybody knows if you tell your wish, it won't come true," I answer.

"You'll have a ball!" they say.

The attendants go all out for us. They bring us Dippity-do hair styling gel and hot rollers, which will actually straighten my naturally curly hair. We get perfume and nail polish and so much trailer trash–blue eye shadow we could start our own mobile park. Then they tell us we don't have to wear the government-issue pajamas and slippers. We can wear our own clothes and our own shoes! We can hear the boys getting ready, too. Their electric shavers whizz, and the smell of Old Spice wafts down the hallway where no fraternizing is allowed. After a dinner of cream chipped beef on toast, we wait in the day rooms for the attendants to escort us down the hallway to the auditorium. When they open the double doors . . . it *is* a night to remember.

The attendants have made stars out of cardboard and spray-painted them with glitter. They hang from the ceiling. It's like we are in the Milky Way. A revolving colored light aimed at the dangling disco ball sends fractured and fragmented rainbows throughout the room. There is a refreshment table piled high with Ho Hos and Twinkies and soda pop punch with melted ice cream on top. There are fresh flowers throughout the room. Each girl is given a corsage, and the boys wear boutonnieres. The band starts to play a brand-new dance.

Giggling, we run into the middle of the room and flail our flaccid muscles like fledglings. And the band plays. We shake it up.

Little Laurie, no bigger than a minute, starts to dance with Big Pete, my favorite attendant. Big Pete is really tall with ice-blue eyes, a Fu Manchu mustache, and a big hanging-over-his-belt gut. Little Laurie puts her shoes on top of his, and they start twisting around the room. Big Debbie is over by the refreshment table sampling each one of the Ho Hos. Carol is clapping her hands and staring at the band: "Boys, boys, boys!" Val snaps her fingers. Shelley scowls, but Sandy is having a blast with her hallucination. Apparently, he is a fabulous conversationalist and quite a good dancer.

Then something starts happening here. The beasts leashed inside of us slip off their collars and come to the ball. And the band plays to all of us wild thangs.

Maybe it's the change of routine or the sugar or the volume of the band or that we are wearing our own clothes or this or that or who knows why, but it all starts breaking apart. Big Debbie harpoons Ho Hos and Twinkies onto her fingers and Hoovers them into her mouth. Carol stares at the boys, claps her hands, and cries, "BOYS, BOYS, BOYS!" Val taps her fist against the window. The fractured and fragmented rainbows act like strobe lights on our fragile nervous systems. Shelley laughs, but Sandy is having too good of a time with her hallucination to notice. The attendants look on at the unintended horror. The band plays while a haze fills our brains.

And me? I do what I still do when confused. I press my back against the wall and fade into the shadows. I look across the room.

I wish, I wish.

The clock strikes twelve. The lead singer grabs the microphone and announces, "Boys, it's that lucky time of the night. Grab that special girl. It's the last dance."

I wish, I wish.

Big Pete leans down and whispers something into George's ear. George is my favorite boy in the boys' ward. He's shaped like an egg. His feet splay out, but his eyes cross in. He rocks back and forth all day long while his hands thump an invisible drum. Every time he gets near me, he engages me in conversation. "Regi, Regi," he insists. "Do you like Pepsi? I like Pepsi. Do you like Pepsi?" I'm pretty sure he likes me. Big Pete pushes George toward me. He rocks his way across the floor.

I wish, I wish.

George stands in front of me and shouts, "Regi, do you want to dance?"

"Yeah!" I gasp. "I do!" I put one hand on his shoulder and another around his pudgy waist. George leans in and wraps his arms around me. He thumps on my back. As my head nestles into his shoulder, he whispers in my ear, "Regi, do you like Pepsi?"

I reply, "Yes, George, I love . . . Pepsi." And the band plays as we climb that stairway to heaven.

Like The Fish and I sing in our sessions now. He reminds me that I have a friend and that there isn't any more room for the pain. One day, he surprises me and says, "If you can graduate from high school, I can get you an all-expenses-paid full scholarship to a four-year college."

"I want to go to music school," I blurt. I didn't know I wanted to until I said it.

"You have to start going to classes."

"I can do it."

"You have to graduate from high school."

"I can do it."

"And, Regi," Like The Fish leans in. "You have to get your mother to sign you out."

"How will I do that?"

Like The Fish just shrugs.

I go to English class every day at three in the afternoon. I love English Man's room. It's big and sunny with deep windowsills. The air is filled with the scent of red and white and pink geraniums. Outside the barred windows, thick icicles diet in the warm spring air. I like

English Man. He's cool. He wears a button-down pastel-pink shirt to school every day. His bangs hang across his forehead like a window valance.

"So, you want to go to college, huh?"

"Yeah, I want to go to music school."

"You have to take the Regents Exam. It's a little bit harder than the regular one."

"That's okay. I was taking the Regents classes before I came here."

"We'll have to read some Shakespeare."

"Did you know my mother loves Shakespeare? And she's very good at word games."

English Man cocks his head to the side and says, "How about a little *Hamlet?*" Sitting across from one another, we take turns reading aloud.

English Man Claudius: "How is it that the clouds still hang on you?"

Regi Hamlet: "O, that this too, too sullied flesh would melt,

Thaw, and resolve itself into a dew,

Or that the Everlasting had not fixed

His canon 'gainst self-slaughter!"

English Man Polonius: ". . . to thine own self be true."

Regi Hamlet: ". . . there is nothing

either good or bad, but thinking makes it so."

———————————————

Like The Fish has a piano delivered and tuned. He tells me I can go down anytime I want. I go down and practice, just a little. I begin conservatively with my scales, major and minor. I knew from a young age that sweetness and sadness were best friends. I pretend to go skiing in Aspen when I practice my arpeggios. I go to the circus when the suspended thirds hop to the sixth to resolve, and I am reminded that the most diminished of us can become whole if we can find a way to take a half step toward the octave. I play the simplest of Bach, Beethoven, a little Chopin, and then *dah, dee, dah, dah dee, dah, dah deee, dah dah*—hopeful.

I begin to tell things to Like The Fish I've never told anyone.

"When I was committed, it wasn't the first time I was here, you know." Like The Fish puts his bony elbows on his bony knees. "I used to come here when I was little. Did you know that? My Grandpa Carpenter was committed to this hospital 'cause there was something funny about him. We used to come visit him some Sundays. It seemed like the sky was so low those days, it rode on the roof of the car. No one said a word the whole car ride. We'd park in front of the Big House, and my dad would sign Grandpa out, and we'd all go to a diner. My parents sat in one booth, and all us kids were in another. My father had his arm around Grandpa's shoulders, fed him with a spoon. Soup dribbled down Grandpa's chin, and my dad wiped it up with a napkin, real sweet. When my parents were paying the bill, my mom always held my dad's hand. Then we'd take Grandpa back to the Big House."

Like The Fish leans in. I go on. "Yeah, the Big House. Y'know— *the Big House.*" I'm panicking now because I realize why I'm telling Like The Fish this story. "If I don't get out of here before I'm eighteen, I'll get transferred over there, and then I'll never get out. My Grandpa Carpenter died in this hospital. I don't want to die in this hospital," I choke out. I hear the St. Lawrence River through the open window. "People say there's something funny about us Carpenter kids." Like The Fish doesn't say anything. His fingers look like church steeples. We just sit in that unadorned room in those two uncomfortable chairs.

––––––––––

English Man and I finish *Hamlet* and move on to *Macbeth*. It's a real laugh fest around here.

Regi Lady Macbeth: "Out, damned spot!"

"When my father was in the full-body cast in the kitchen, I couldn't sleep at night, so I used to get up and fill a bucket with boiling water and Spic and Span. I'd get a scrub brush and go into the bathroom and scrub the sink and the tub and the toilet, and if I wasn't tired yet, I'd scrub the ceiling and the walls and the floor. Then I'd dry them with a towel, and if I still wasn't tired, I'd do it again. I'd do it until I was tired, but by the time I was tired, it was usually time to go to school. I wanted to talk to somebody. I wanted to talk to my mother, but my mother didn't want to talk to me. I don't know why." I choke back my tears.

Like The Fish just listens in that quiet, unadorned room in those two uncomfortable chairs.

I get a letter from my friend Dawn:

> *Dear Regi,*
>
> *Kendra got pregnant on the night of the prom and she and Steve aren't sure they're gonna keep the baby, but if they do keep it they're probably gonna get married in their senior year. Isn't that cool? If it's a boy, they're gonna name it Steve, after, y'know, Steve. If it's a girl, they don't know what they're gonna call it. I hope you're doing good.*
>
> *Luv ya, xoxoxoxoxo*

She includes a picture she has drawn of a horse. It's very realistic except for the pastels. I hang it over my bed. I want to go home. I write my mother a letter.

Though this be madness, yet there is
method in 't.

Dear Mom,

To be, or not to be?

I am very sorry for everything I have done.

Whether 'tis nobler in the mind to suffer

The slings and arrows of outrageous fortune . . .

I know now that it is my fault I am here and that my choices hurt you and Dad.

Or to take arms against a sea of troubles . . .

I would like to come home for a visit, if it's okay with you.

And, by opposing, end them?

I promise to be good. Love, Regi.

She takes me home for the weekend. I'm quiet, and I don't make any trouble, so she lets me stay an extra day. I go home on a Friday and come back on a Sunday. Then it's back on a Monday, then a Tuesday, and then one Wednesday, my mother says, "We've had a meeting and decided to sign you out, but if you aren't good, I'm going to sign you right back in."

Regi Witches: "Double, double toil and trouble;
    Fire burn and cauldron bubble . . ."

I graduate from eleventh and twelfth grade. I turn eighteen, and no one can sign me in to anything. I apply to Ithaca College School of Music. I am accepted. I graduate. I get married. I have kids. I get divorced. I have one of those wonderful, turbulent lives, just like everybody else. We never speak of the hospital, and for thirty-five years, the story lies silent within me. We never talk about it until my mother is dying.

I am standing next to her hospital bed when suddenly her bright blue eyes pop open and she grabs my forearm.

"I don't know how you made it out of there. It must have been awful. I signed you in to save your life, you know. To save your life!" she says desperately.

"I know, Mom. Thank you." Her eyes close, and she falls back asleep.

What I also know, but I don't think my mother knew, was that signing me in saved her life and my father's life, and I am eternally grateful for that.

I look at my mother. Her skin is gray. I love her. I sit with her, holding her hand, counting the number of breaths from the oxygen machine, as we maneuver through the labyrinth of life and death.

Who knows why girls go crazy? I went.

What do I know? There is nothing either good or bad, but thinking makes it so.

Me, Moses, and the Dog

Mom slurs, then slumps, and is finally saved by the ambulance men. Mary, Dad, and I stand around her bed in the emergency room. My mother's face is pale and clammy. I watch her eyes sail back and forth beneath closed lids. I remember her eyelashes brushing my cheek as we lay in the grass outside of Grandma Carpenter's house. "This is how a butterfly kisses," she whispered to me. I hold her hand with the small scar above the knuckle and smooth back her gray, sweaty hair. She once paid me a penny for each gray hair I could pluck out when her hair was brown and thick and musky smelling. The room has only four people in it, but it's crowded with memories of the closeness of childhood and the chasm that we never bridged after I was released from Southwood. The air is filled with the sound of blips and beeps and oxygen pump whooshes. My worried father holds her hand and tells us stories.

"The secret to a good navy bean soup, Reg, is onions. You need a lot of onions to make the soup taste good. And black pepper. That's how my mother made it. Every Friday night, Mother would make a big pot of navy bean soup and bread for anybody who came over for the card game. We played Penny a Pitch with the neighbors every Friday. Mother used to get so mad at Dad when he played the wrong card. 'What did you play *that* for?' she'd rail at him and slam her fist down on the table. Mother was a card shark, and she hated to lose her pennies."

Dad tells us stories we have heard a thousand times before. "You kids and your mother and I were driving across country from California to Clayton when I picked up a sailor to help me with the driving. Your mother couldn't drive then. 'Hey, buddy,' I asked him, 'could you drive through the night and wake me up in the morning?' So he did, and I did, and when I woke up, I asked him, 'Where the hell are we?' 'We're about a mile from my house,' said that sailor." His stories comfort and calm us.

"Somewhere around ten o'clock on Friday night, Uncle Nils used to stagger up Theresa Street, drunker than a skunk, singing at the top of his lungs. 'Let me call you sweetheart.' Uncle Nils would stop and stare up at the lamppost, weaving back and forth, then knock on that post and say, 'Let me in, darlin'. I know you're up there. I see your light on.'" Dad laughs right out loud at this memory.

That afternoon in the hospital, I learn what people talk about when people they love are dying: soup, onions, relatives, card games. Nothing in particular.

"The secret to a good navy bean soup, Reg, is a lot of onions."

When my mother awakes, Mary, Dad, and I are standing at her bedside.

"Hi, Mom," I say as I smooth the hair away from her forehead. "Do you know my name?" I ask her.

"You're Regina," she says so sweetly and smiles at me.

"That's right." I am so happy she knows my name, my real name. She is the only one who ever calls me Regina.

"Now who's that?" I ask and point to Mary.

"That's the dog."

We laugh uncomfortably.

"And who's this handsome man, Mom?" I ask and shift my gaze to our father.

"That?" she asks, wide eyed. "That's Moses!" She throws her head back and cackles. Our eyebrows go up, and we look at one another uneasily. "Is that my brother Johnny?" she asks inquisitively. I follow her gaze into the empty hallway. Johnny has been dead for forty years. Is the angel of death disguised as a WWII soldier? Is this a holy visitation or a hallucination? We wait and wonder, watching her drift in and out of lucidity. She's had a stroke, the doctor tells us. Not a bad one, but she will need to stay in the hospital while she recovers. "Her delusions will lessen, and she'll be normal again," the doctor reassures us. I haven't put the words *normal* and *my mother* into the same sentence for quite a while.

Her body recovers, but her mind is like a tangled string with too many knots in it.

The doctor recommends we transfer her from the hospital into a rehabilitation home. The beds are laid out barracks-style, and the white sheets make them look like albino dominoes. She's wheelchair-bound now and needs help dressing and bathing and toileting. Her face is lopsided, with one droopy eye and a tired mouth. This woman has nowhere to go now except the foxhole of her mind.

"I have cancer of the sphincter, you know," she announces casually as I push her wheelchair to the dining hall one day.

"Does Mom have cancer of the sphincter?" I ask Mary later.

"No. I'm not even sure anyone can get cancer of the sphincter."

———————————

When Mom becomes wheelchair-bound, we get her a four-speed, electric, horsepowered chariot to maneuver her new equally tall and wide five-by-five-foot frame. She has always hoarded food, but now she steals it from people's rooms, meal carts, drawers, and even hands if someone dozes mid-bite. When someone tries to stop her, she turns the chair up to four and hits their wheelchair, making it scatter like a cue ball on a pool table.

Her rants continue.

"Ha-ha! Did you see that man with his crack hanging out?"

"The CIA is coming to get me. They know I killed Oswald."

"I couldn't sleep last night, so I watched porn. The priest spread his semen all over the countryside . . . again."

"The blue of that paper is the same as the blue on that bird. They are sharing thoughts, but I can hear them. They think I can't, but I can."

"Shut up, ya old geezer," she sneers to a man bold enough to say something she didn't like. Who is this woman? Not my mother. My mother quoted Shakespeare and corrected my grammar.

"You're just a loser waiting to win," she taunts a woman who accidentally sits in her chair at bingo one afternoon.

Her delusions become stranger.

"Regina, are you blind?"

"No, I'm not blind, Mom."

"Oh yes you are," she informs me.

Her delusions become more troubling.

"Your father's a murderer. He murdered your brother. That's how he died."

"Stop it, Mom. Tim died in a car crash. Stop it now."

And more heartbreaking.

"I'm afraid I'm going to miss it," she cries one day as we look out of the window at a flock of gathering birds.

"Miss what?" I ask.

"I'm going to miss all the beauty before I go," she says wistfully.

"I'm afraid of that too, Mom," I reply.

Who is the woman living inside my mother's body? Is she butterfly-kisses-in-the-grass mother, wiping-me-down-with-rubbing-al-cohol-when-I-had-scarlet-fever mother, bought-me-a-piano mother, or I'll-never-sign-you-out-of-Southwood frozen mother? Who is my real mother?

"Are you blind, Regina?"

I come every day now, determined to decipher her code. If only I listen more carefully or pay more attention, I will find my real mother. I begin writing down my mother's ramblings, sure that the characters and stories tumbling out of her will eventually make perfect sense.

"Carla eats eyeballs. When you wear that shirt, the top half of your body is invisible. Don't sit under the apple tree with anyone else but me, no, no, no. This teddy bear doesn't have any bones. Poor teddy. Regina, are you blind?"

Every day I wait for her to take me to "once upon a time" or to "in the beginning." I want her to bring me to the perfect place where nothing bad happens and everything is forgiven and understood. The place where things make sense. Where she makes sense.

"I remember the first date I had with your father. We screwed all night up in the balcony of the movie!" It never happens. Her stories never make sense. My mother is a letter written in a secret code in an unsealed envelope. She never makes sense.

I do her nails and comb her hair. I rub cream on her cracked heels. I don't come as often as I should or can.

One afternoon, my unpredictable mother surprises me. "You know, we just never had a chance to bond properly. You were taken from me because they thought you were going to die. They used to do that then. I had to let that woman take care of you for six months because I couldn't do it. I wasn't allowed to see you or take care of you until I could stand up without help. They didn't know I was leaning against the wall when they brought you to me. They thought I was better. As soon as they left, I fell down, but they let me keep you. I got you back."

Regina, are you blind?

The Lord works in mysterious ways. *She* is the womb in which I grew. The veil present at birth slowly lifts, and she is revealed to me. My real mother is the one in front of me speaking to her spirits. She is my butterfly-kisses-I'm-never-signing-you-out-How-do-I-love-thee?-Let-me-count-the-ways mother. I am her butterfly-kisses-crazy-running-away-piano-playing-I-hate-you-I'm-sorry-I-did-my-best daughter.

Do I have a mother? Do I have a child?

Those questions spirited between us at birth are answered.

Regina Coeli, O Queen of Heaven, rejoice: alleluia;
For the child whom you so nobly bore: alleluia;
Rose from the dead, as he foretold: alleluia;
Pray for us now, we ask of you: alleluia.

I Love You; Will You Bury Me?

Clayton is a small town, but we've got a big cemetery. Tall spires and stone angels silently testify the names I've heard my whole life: Garnsey, Wingerath, Kehoe, Black, Sullivan, Natali, Hunt, Riddler, and Carpenter. These are the same names my father grew up hearing, and his father and his father before that. The Clayton cemetery is filled with the remains of generations of families who, like us, have lived and died in Clayton for hundreds of years. It's almost as if each generation of a family is like a wave on the St. Lawrence River. The eldest generation crests and crashes, and the next generation rolls forward to take its place. This is the natural order of things. Everyone expects it to happen. We Carpenters expected it to, too. We just didn't expect it to happen the way that it did.

It took my Aunt Margeurite several hours to realize my Uncle Eddard wasn't dozing—he was dead. "That man never did talk much," she said in her own defense.

My Uncle Rip died of a heart attack. When warned by his doctor to give up those fatty meat soppings, he declared, "Doctor, I'd rather die!" So he did.

My Aunt Dot died like we all hope to, asleep in her own bed at an old age.

But later on when my Uncle Joe died, his death marked the passing of my father's entire Carpenter generation.

Eddard, Dot, Bernie, Rip, Joe, and my father, Carl Carpenter, were all born on a small farm on Clayton Center Road in Clayton, New York, and raised during the Great Depression. They were all graduates of St. Mary's Catholic School, and they all saw the beginning and the end of World War II. Each and every one of them— Eddard, Dot, Bernie, Rip, Joe, and my father, Carl Carpenter—said "til death do us part" just once.

Bernie and Hub sittin' in a tree,
K-I-S-S-I-N-G.
First comes love,
then comes marriage;
no little babies in their baby carriage.

After high school graduation, Aunt Bernie fled small-town life to seek her fame and fortune in the wilds of Miami, Florida. While working as a secretary, she met a widower named Hub and married him. After a long marriage, he died and she became a widow. Then she became a wandering widow. Finally, she became a forgetful and fragile wandering widow walking miles away from home and being escorted back home by concerned neighbors and police officers. My father took her in. She died in the back bedroom of his house.

Aunt Bernie had taken care of most of her own funeral arrangements. She wanted to be cremated and have her remains put into a lovely bronze box, which I carried to the grave site. She also specified that she wanted her remains to be buried next to her husband, Hub. Hub, however, had specified that he wanted to be buried next to his first wife. Aunt Bernie got around that awkward complication by buying the plot on the other side and having a tombstone engraved with capital letters: *TIL DEATH DO US PART.* (On cold nights, I like to imagine Uncle Hub's eternity sandwiched between those two women.) Uncle Joe and Dad insisted on taking care of the remaining arrangements, and we let them, out of respect, even though they were getting a little dotty.

It was a scent-filled spring day when we all assembled at the grave site. The cemetery representative was there wearing a slightly wrinkled pair of black pants and a crumpled white shirt. His red comb-over kept getting caught in the wind and whirling up like a cyclone. His nametag read *Cemetery Representative.*

"Mr. Carpenter, what time are you expecting the priest?" CR asked my father discreetly.

"Joe, what time are you expecting the priest?" Dad asked his brother.

"How would I know? I thought you were gonna call the priest," was his bewildered response.

"You said *you* were gonna call the priest! Oh, for God's sake," my father muttered. Turning back to the cemetery representative, he declared, "We decided against the priest."

"Oh, well, I could read the Lord's Prayer, if you like," he volunteered.

"At these prices, that's the least you could do," mumbled my father.

But my suspicions were aroused. *Read* the Lord's Prayer? What? Catholics don't read the Lord's Prayer! It's tattooed upon our souls at the moment of conception and springs forth, fully formed, on the day of our First Communion. *Read* the Lord's Prayer? Who was this guy? Why was he at my Aunt Bernie's funeral? And what had Aunt Bernie done during her life to deserve him at her funeral? My suspicions were confirmed when CR mangled the entire prayer, even saying "And lead us into temptation!"

"Amen!" cried my father a little too exuberantly. Then CR pulled back the Astroturf and revealed the burial hole. It felt unholy to drop a box with a relative's remains into what looked like a golf hole, but I did it as ceremoniously as I could. When I looked up, CR was gone and there was a thin wisp of smoke in the air. Without the priest to close things out, we really didn't know what to do. We just stood around shifting our weight from one foot to another. Finally, Cousin Cathy saved us.

"Why don't we tell some stories about Aunt Bernie as a eulogy?" she suggested.

"Great idea! Okay!" we all agreed.

"I'll go first," Cathy said. "When I was a freshman in college, I visited Aunt Bernie in Miami for spring break. Aunt Bernie told me to put everything into the convertible and we would go to the beach. Uncle Hub was dead by then. Well, we got to this beautiful beach with white sand and big waves. It was just gorgeous. Aunt Bernie stood up on the driver's seat and looked around and then said, 'No, honey, we don't want this beach.' I thought, *Why not? What's wrong with this beach?* We went to another beach, and she said the same thing: 'No, no, not this one.' I started wondering, *Am I ever going to get to the beach?* Finally, we pulled into one with an all-male soccer team oiled up and playing in their Speedos. 'Grab your stuff, honey. This is the beach we want,' Aunt Bernie winked."

"She used to ride our donkey to school and feed it at lunchtime," remembered Uncle Joe.

When it was my turn, a deep sense of shame roiled through my body. "One time, when Aunt Bernie was visiting, she caught me on Aunt Violet's porch. She held my face in her hands and stared at my mouth for a long time. She told me I had a thin upper lip just like her, and if I ever wanted to have a boy kiss me, I would have to paint an upper lip on with red lipstick like she did. Then she commanded me to look at her upper lip. When I lifted my eyes to the space underneath her nostrils, all I saw was this big red smear, and red lipstick was creeping up her wrinkles toward her eyes. It looked like she had blood poisoning. It was . . . spooky," I whispered.

"She sure could hold her beer, huh?" said Cindi.

Then it was my father's turn. I'd like to think it was the grief that made him say it, but it was probably due to his own inappropriate sense of social boundaries.

"That woman was the biggest miser I ever met in my life!" he yelled and threw his arms into the air. The awkward silence was interrupted only by the sound of her box turning over in its grave.

"Let's eat!" cried Aunt Bev.

Joe and Bev sittin' in a tree,
K-I-S-S-I-N-G.
First comes love,
then comes marriage;
two little girls in their baby carriage.

Uncle Joe was my father's next oldest and closest brother. They shared a bedroom and a bed until they both went into the war. While my father was crawling on his belly in the Philippines for the Army, Uncle Joe was flying and fixing airplanes for the Air Force. Joe was at the Battle of Midway and the bombing of Pearl Harbor. Those brothers were so close, they even got married the same year, 1946, and those women officially became Carpenters. My father married a girl from out in California, while my Uncle Joe stayed a little bit closer to home and married a girl from Strawberry Lane. He married a Riddler girl: Bev Riddler.

Ah, Bev Riddler. No amount of military training could have adequately prepared Uncle Joe for life with Aunt Bev. She was a thick-waisted, big-bosomed, chain-smoking woman given to negative proclamations such as "Huh!" and "Oh, honey! I could tell you a few stories, especially about your Aunt Bernie during the war!"

Later on, when she got emphysema, she was tethered to her chair by miles of clear plastic tubing connected to an oxygen machine that delivered her air in three-quarter-waltz time. Uncle Joe doted on her. He did the laundry, the cooking, and the cleaning. He brought her the paper and her coffee, and, of course, he answered the telephone, which they kept in the front hallway next to the oxygen machine. Did I mention Uncle Joe was almost stone-cold deaf? It happened gradually over the course of the marriage. When the phone rang, he had to turn off the oxygen machine to hear the person on the other end, and I have to tell you that it was kind of a guilty pleasure to watch Aunt Bev sputter and spew and turn shades of blue even Picasso hadn't imagined. Don't worry; her skin tone evened out once he turned the oxygen machine back on.

Those negative proclamations eventually gave way to the most plaintive and piteous of cries.

"Joe? Joe? Are you there?"

Uncle Joe was always there, taking care of things, reading his paper, or petting his dachshund. When Aunt Bev died, she was buried with her people, the Riddlers, and was deeply mourned by my Uncle Joe.

Carl and Josie sittin' in a tree,
K-I-S-S-I-N-G.
First comes love,
then comes marriage;
five little babies in their baby carriage.

Everybody expected my mother to go first, but my father took a turn for the worse, so we put him into the same nursing home as my mother, where they were cared for by angels with Jamaican accents earning minimum wage. His decline started typically. There was the wandering and the forgetting, the sleeping in other people's beds. There was the incessant "You got a butt?"

"You don't smoke anymore, Dad."

"Since when?" he scoffed.

"Since you were standing next to the fireplace wearing an oxygen tank trying to light a cigarette," I explained.

"Ah, pfft," he waved his hand dismissively. "You got a butt?" he asked.

My father was a proud man. He endured countless operations on his legs after he was discharged from the army in 1946. At the age of fifty-three, when they fused both his legs so they couldn't bend, he was one hundred percent disabled. Each operation left him in a wheelchair until he was strong enough to walk with crutches. Then he'd switch to a cane, and once he was steady again, he'd throw the cane away. His gait resembled a plastic wind-up toy. Dad hated being in his wheelchair and said he would rather die than be in it. One day, I came to visit, and he was tucked under a blanket in the wheelchair. His legs stuck out in front of him like railroad ties. I knew we were walking down a road together but I would be the only one walking back. I leaned in and kissed him.

"Hi, Dad." I smiled.

Do I know you? replied the look in his eyes as he pulled back and scanned my face. Then he leaned in and kissed me a little too long. "How much do they pay for it around here?" he whispered and looked at my breasts.

"Too much, Dad, way too much," I told him.

By my next visit, he had climbed out of the wheelchair and into his bed and fallen into a coma. He lay outstretched on the bed, and his face was like a death mask: eyes sunken, skin taut, breath like a scraping death rattle. My mother tootled in, her heels acting like pistons propelling her wheelchair forward.

"Carl! Carl! I'm going to bingo!" she announced.

"Why are you going to bingo, Mom? It isn't for three more hours."

"I don't want to lose my spot!"

"You can't lose your spot, Mom. It's a round table."

"Oh, pfft," she said, waved her hand dismissively, and turned her attention back to Dad. "Carl! Carl! I've got a joke for you. How did the mortician propose to his girlfriend? Give up? He asked her, 'I love you. Will you bury me?'" Turning back to me, she said, "He looks better." She tootled out.

Once alone with my father, I saw he did not look better.

When my father was young, he was quite a dandy. His wavy black hair was pomaded until it was flammable and styled to look like a cresting tsunami. The mustache he had been born wearing was trimmed and combed daily. His baby-smooth cheeks reeked of Aqua Velva. His nails were always perfectly manicured. His legs were long and lanky. His muscular shoulders tapered down to such a narrow waist that he looked like a stingray. In the summer, his skin was bronze. But now, his black hair had turned the color of silver moonlight and clung greasily to his scalp and neck—an old man's hair. His mustache and cheeks were half stubble and half shorn. His nails were jagged and dirty. His hands smelled like rotting meat.

"You've got a big trip coming up, Dad, a big trip. I'm going to get you ready," I whispered in his ear.

I took down the purple plastic bucket from the shelf next to his bed, filled it with warm water in the bathroom sink, swirled in some antiseptic soap, then dropped in one of those thin hospital washcloths. I covered Dad's privates with a towel and removed his hospital gown.

My father's body could have doubled for Frankenstein's monster. He had been pinched, poked, perforated, stitched, sewn, and stapled since the time he was a twenty-two-year-old soldier until the last day of his life. The long scar that ran from his navel to his clavicle reminded me of his four heart surgeries. The scars on either side of his belly were from his bladder cancer, and his hairless, shiny legs were covered with scars made by scalpels: straight scars, intersecting scars, and half moon–shaped scars. Each scar was a reminder of a bone or a joint or a fragment of his body doctors deemed expendable and then discarded. Those scars were also the ruts in the road my family walked down in pain and violence and fear and forgiveness and love.

"You've got a big trip coming up, Dad," I whispered again.

I washed his chest and arms. I ran the washcloth over his hips and buttocks and down his legs. I washed his feet. I filed his nails and shaved him, then dabbed on some Aqua Velva. I covered his body in baby powder and dressed him in a fresh robe. As I drew the washcloth through his moonlight-silver hair, big clumps fell out and shimmered on top of the water.

"Now you're ready, Dad. You're all ready."

My father waited politely for me to leave before dying. As I sat in the green chair in my living room that evening, I felt a whoosh fly through the top of my head and out my toes. A phone call a few minutes later told me what I already knew. The sun had fallen from the heavens.

We discovered my mother's cancer about a month later. It was too advanced for the treatments to do any good, but she insisted on having them anyway even though they burned her skin and made her hair fall out. We got her a big bouffant, Marilyn Monroe–blond wig. "It goes with my mustache!" she cried.

I had been singing with a hospice choir around that time, and I asked them if they would come sing to my mother before she died. I thought I had a few more days with her, but when we arrived, it was clear to everyone except me that this was the day. We held hands and encircled her bed. "Deep peace of the running wave to you," we sang. They kept singing, and I crawled into bed with my mother. I wrapped my arms and legs around her bloated body. She smelled like a chocolate éclair. A phone call later that evening told me that the moon had fallen from the heavens too.

My parents were plain people. They wanted to be cremated and put into plain brown boxes. It was a hot, sunny summer day when we assembled at the grave site. We didn't want a priest, so we said the *Our Father* by ourselves. I pulled back the Astroturf and revealed the burial hole. After that, I placed the boxes in as ceremoniously as I could. Before the funeral, I asked my brothers and sisters, "Do you mind if I keep some of the ashes out so I can give them a water burial?" No, none of them minded. It had taken years for my parents to die, and by then everyone was so tired they just went home. I went down to the St. Lawrence River.

Standing on the town docks, I watched the sparkling waves. In my mind's eye, I imagined I was sprinkling my parents' ashes onto the top of the water where the current picked them up and whisked them out to sea, all while a string orchestra played "What's it all about, Alfie?" I stepped off the dock and into the water. Before opening the Ziploc bag, I said the *Our Father*:

Our Father, who art in heaven,
hallowed be thy name.
Thy kingdom come,
thy will be done
on earth, as it is in heaven.
Give us this day our daily bread,
and forgive us our trespasses,
as we forgive those who trespass against us,
and lead us not into temptation,
but deliver us from evil.
Amen.

I sprinkled my parents' ashes onto the top of the water where, much to my horror, they sunk like stones and covered my legs like cement boots. *Ach! I am wearing my parents!* Just then, a pair of mallard ducks swam up to me.

"Quack, quack, quack," they laughed and swam around me. Their webbed feet churned up the water, the ashes lifted, and the current picked them up and carried them out to the sea. As the ducks swam away, they looked over their winged shoulders and "quack, quack, quack." Ah, my parents were a real couple of kidders.

A few years later, Uncle Joe died exactly as he lived, without ceremony or fanfare. As they lowered his ornate bronze coffin into the ground next to Aunt Bev, we intoned the *Our Father* with the priest. A 21-gun salute rang out, and "Taps" was played. Uncle Joe was getting the veteran's funeral every veteran deserves. It was a cold, windy November day when we said our good-byes to the last member of my father's generation: Eddard, Dot, Bernie, Rip, Joe, and my father, Carl Carpenter. They crested and crashed, and my generation rolled forward to take their place: Wendy, Cindi, Mary, Cathy, Patty, David, and Regi.

Til death do us part.

Fanned by a
Southwest Breeze

The fire sirens wake us from our sleep, and like mice we scurry out of our houses to see what calamity has befallen one of us. Our overcoats hide wrinkled pajamas and nightgowns. We wear slippers instead of shoes. Hats cover messy bed-tousled hair. The smell of burning wood makes us pull our collars up over our mouths as we run toward the burning house on Riverside Drive next to Mercier's Boat Yard. The blazing house crackles and smokes while the front porch windowpanes shatter and spray shards of glass across the street. The entire town is here. I grab my father's cool, smooth hand. The other children hang onto a parent's coat sleeve or pant leg. We all huddle together silently with wide eyes to watch the house, once the color of sunshine, being engulfed in flames. The firemen spray arcs of water like rainbows onto the roof in vain. The river, blue by day and black by night, flows by indifferent to the disaster, while embers fly upward and drop through the air like red snowflakes.

"They lost the pictures, even the pictures," the adults murmur. As if nothing else mattered.

I am nine years old sitting next to my father in the rocking chair of our living room. He's smoking a corncob pipe. Carter's Special Tobacco Blend tickles my nose. We are holding a photo album in our lap.

My father is showing me two portraits side by side.

"Who are they?" I ask him.

"They," he says and takes a toke off his pipe, "are my mother's parents." The man has black hair, a handlebar mustache, and a black bowtie. He looks like an undertaker. The woman has ice-blue eyes and a collar rolled up to her bottom lip.

"They were German. We visited them every Sunday. We couldn't speak unless spoken to. Lucky for us, they only spoke German and we didn't. They believed in 'children are to be seen and not heard,' not like you rugrats." I smile and make a face at him.

Underneath the photograph, someone has written *married 56 years Thursday, Mr. and Mrs. John Knapp, 1929.*

Dad points to the black-and-white photograph of a woman with raccoon eyes and a wide-lapelled dress. She's standing in front of a small stucco house with a screened-in front porch. She's smiling thoughtfully into the camera. "Your Grandma Carpenter was an angel," he says wistfully. I lick my lollipop. "My father bought that house on Union Street during the Depression. It cost $1,500. Pop worked as an elevator operator at the Woodruff Hotel in Watertown during the week."

"What did your mother do?"

"She took care of us six kids, chickadee!

"Pop was a customs agent at the coal docks on the weekends," my father continues. "Your Uncle Joe and I used to shovel coal into the cargo of the ships when they came to the town dock to fill up. We jumped in and shoveled like mad while the coal poured out the chute."

"Wasn't that kind of dangerous? Couldn't you have been buried alive underneath the coal?"

"Well, yeah, but where else are ya gonna earn a quarter an hour?" my father says and shakes his head at me.

He turns the page, and now I see a photo of Grandma Carpenter standing in the dappled shade of two large oak trees. Beneath the trees are two white rocking chairs waiting for their next customers. The river rolls by in the background. Its waves jump and splash like dolphins.

"The garden is off to the left. You can't see it here. Pretty much everything we ate came from the garden. When she planted corn, I dropped a fish head in the hole to make it grow better."

"Ew," I say and wrinkle my nose.

"Ew yourself. It tasted good."

The bottom of the picture reads *Agnes Knapp Carpenter, 1936.*

My father taps the next picture with his index finger. "That's Rip, Violet, Junior, Dot, Frank, Bernie, Hub, and Bev." These are most of my Carpenter relatives before I knew them. They're young, slender, and smiling. Uncle Rip looks dapper in his dark pinstripe suit. A small stuffed bird perches on the brim of Aunt Violet's white hat. Uncle Rip's arm is draped around her shoulder. Cousin Junior stands in front of Aunt Violet, and her hands rest comfortably on his shoulders. Junior is around six and wears a white T-shirt and a Navy cap too big for him. The gap where his front teeth used to be looks like a tunnel for his tongue. Aunt Dot and Uncle Frank stand in line next to Aunt Bernie and Uncle Hub. They're wearing their Sunday finest: suits, hats, and carnations on their lapels. Their smiles are broad and full of uneven teeth. Aunt Bev is standing slightly off by herself. Her husband, Uncle Joe, is still in Hawaii. "That's the day I came home from the war," my father says. "Uncle Joe was still in Pearl Harbor. You know he was eatin' a piece of your grandmother's fruitcake when the bombs hit?" The bottom of the frame says *1945.*

"Why aren't there any pictures of us on the other side of town near Goose Bay?" I ask.

"That's not our side of town. We're Frenchies. We live on the river. Our side of town used to be called French Town because that's what the priests spoke when they came here from Canada," my father explains.

He stops looking at the photo album and looks into space instead. A smile spreads across his face like butter on warm toast. "In the wintertime, the firemen used to come over to French Town and hose down the hill on Alexandria Street so we could go sledding." I picture what he's telling me in my mind. I see him bundled up with a sled rushing down Alexandria Street, crossing over Mary Street, and sliding straight onto the river like a hockey puck to its goal. His face is all scrunched up because he's smiling so hard.

"Are there any pictures of you when you were a kid?" I ask.

"Nah," he says.

"Why not?"

"I was a rotten kid," he shrugs.

"Who told you that?"

"Everybody. Everybody knew I was a rotten kid."

"What made you rotten?"

"Born that way. That's what my father said."

As an adult, I looked for another story of my father. I asked his childhood friends what they remembered about my dad.

"Your father was a great baseball player. He coulda played for the Yankees if the war hadna come along. Too bad about his legs."

"He taught old Jim Sullivan to read by having him read the Sunday funny papers."

"There used to be a woman named Millie who worked at the Boat Line. She was a deaf-mute. She sold trinkets, like plastic coin purses, dolls made from shells, pencils, stuff like that. She couldn't speak a word, only point and grunt. Your father stood there and listened to her and nodded his head. You know, I think he actually understood her."

"Well, let's see. I've been in this wheelchair since I got polio when I was three. Your father used to pick me up in the morning and carry me to school, and if I had to change classes, he and the other guys would pick me up and carry me there too. Your Dad even put me on the train to NYC after we graduated from high school. He said to me, 'Les, how are you gonna get around New York without a wheelchair?' I told him, 'Just put me on the train, Carl. I'll figure it out.' And he did, and I had a great time."

Back in the chair of my childhood, we continue to turn the pages and look at pictures in succession.

Snapshot: *Couple wed 36 years—November 29, 1941.* Grandma and Grandpa Carpenter are smiling at the camera. Her white hair is combed to the side. He's wearing a wide tie and she a floral-print dress. His arm is wrapped around her, and her arm embraces his waist. They look nice. I wonder if they were. Would she bake cookies and tuck me in under handmade quilts? Would Grandpa give me piggy-back rides and read to me? Would it be perfect?

Snapshot: Grandma and Grandpa Carpenter are standing next to one another, their shoulders touching. Grandma smiles, while Grandpa stares thin-lipped and icy at the camera. *1951* someone has written.

Newspaper article: Grandma and Grandpa are older now. He's wearing a white short-sleeve shirt and a belt around his thick middle. She is standing slightly behind him. Her hand is curled around his elbow. I can see the oak trees in the background. The caption reads: *Golden Anniversary—Mr. and Mrs. Benjamin Carpenter, Clayton, will celebrate their 50th wedding anniversary Tuesday, 1955. Mrs. Carpenter is the former Agnes Knapp.*

Snapshot: Grandpa Carpenter is in the middle of the photograph. Grandma is to his right wearing a sweater with holes in it. Her hair is pinned up like a cinnamon bun on the top of her head. There are dark circles around her sunken eyes. Some of her front teeth are missing, and the ones remaining are slanting to one side or another. Aunt Bernie is on the left wearing a stylish hat and lapel pin. In the background is a long wooden structure where Grandpa lives at the St. Lawrence Psychiatric Hospital. The clouds are dark and match the mood in his eyes.

Pasted onto the page is a newspaper article. It's yellowed and worn on the edges. The image is slightly distorted because of age and wear.

Watertown Daily News, Trapped by Flames May 7, 1960

Mrs. Agnes K. Carpenter, 73, and Sharon Sheley, 17, Dead—Fire Starts in Stovepipe (Special to the Times)

"Tell it to me again. Tell me again," I beg my father.

"It was in the middle of the night. I woke up to the sirens," he says patiently. "Then I got a phone call from Mrs. LaLonde."

"The Mrs. LaLonde who used to curl her hair around her ears to make them look like telephone receivers? That Mrs. LaLonde?" I ask.

"Yuh. She told me to get over to my mother's house. I ran over to Union Street, and when I got there, the house was on fire. Your grandma died in the fire along with the girl next door who stayed overnight with her. That white ceramic castle was in her fishbowl. That's all we have left of Grandma. That and the photographs," my father tells me for the umpteenth time.

Whenever my father tells me the story, I imagine walking over to the empty plot on Union Street where the house stood. The house's frame is forgotten, but the horseradish root in the garden is still growing. Aunt Violet digs it up in the springtime and grinds it into a pulp. Tears run down her cheeks.

There's something about the story that won't let go of me.

"Tell it to me again."

"It was in the middle of the night. I woke up to the sirens," he says patiently. "Then I got a phone call from Mrs. LaLonde. She told me to get over to my mother's house. I ran over to Union Street, and when I got there, the house was on fire. Your grandma died in the fire along with the girl next door who stayed overnight with her. That white ceramic castle was in her fishbowl. That's all we have left of Grandma. That and the photographs," he repeats almost robotically. Then a new piece of the puzzle slips into place. My mother bustles into the living room with a wet dishtowel in her hands and overhears my father telling the story.

"Oh, we were so lucky! We could have lost your sister Mary. Your grandmother invited her to stay that night, but I said no, thank God! We could have lost your sister," she repeats, wringing her hands on the towel. My father's lips go white. I snuggle closer to him.

The glossy white ceramic castle sits on the bookcase. You would never know it had been through such a terrible tragedy.

Clayton Woman, Girl Suffocate in House Fire. Fire Tragedy Scene— Mrs. Agnes Knapp Carpenter, 74, and Miss Sharon Sheley, 17, both of Clayton, died of suffocation early this morning when fire ran through Mrs. Carpenter's frame stucco covered residence at 815 Union Street at 4:02 a.m. Sharon Sheley, daughter of Mr. and Mrs. Perry Sheley, 814 Rees Street, Clayton, resided with Mrs. Carpenter, whose husband Benjamin Carpenter is hospitalized in Ogdensburg.

I have only two real memories of my Grandfather Carpenter. I am eight, and we are driving along Route 12 toward Ogdensburg. The St. Lawrence River is narrow here and looks muddy. It's springtime and raining. The clouds hitchhike a ride on our roof. I am in the way back of the car playing with my plastic Bendable Barbie. She twists and turns to the song on the radio. Her long blond hair whips out behind her. We turn off the main highway and into the St. Lawrence Psychiatric Hospital. There are lots of long ornate buildings and lush green lawns. The buildings have dark red shingles and green roofs. My father parks in front of one of the biggest buildings and goes inside. He returns with an old man with a big nose, pointy chin, big ears, and drooping earlobes. He looks like my dad. The old man is shuffling along while my father guides him to the car. My mother gets out of the car and the old man gets in. My mother buckles his seatbelt and slides in next to him. We go to a diner, and I watch my father spoon-feed this old man. "A little more soup for ya, Pop?" my father asks and wipes his chin as the soup dribbles down. The next memory is when I am ten. The old man is in a dark navy suit in a coffin at Cummings Funeral Home. His hair is combed and parted neatly on the side. His skin looks too rosy, like he's made of plastic. Uncle Joe, Aunt Bernie, Aunt Dot, Uncle Rip, Aunt Bev, and Aunt Violet are all there. No one is speaking.

"Tell me about Grandpa Carpenter," I ask my siblings. I am an adult now and trying to make sense of the fire and who I come from. Each of them has a story to tell.

"He lived with us when you were really little," says one.

"He wouldn't take his medicine. We were afraid of him," says another.

"He wandered around town in his pajamas," remembers another.

"He was scary and mean. He said we were rotten," is the last memory told to me.

"Dad, can I have your permission to get Grandpa's records from the hospital?"

"Yeah, I guess so," he says and shrugs.

They send me his death certificate in a plain white envelope: Benjamin Carpenter, Clayton, deceased. Heart disease. Schizophrenic. Dr. Fawkes, my hometown doctor, is the coroner.

"I took him in as long as I could, but your mother wouldn't have it after a while. She said he wasn't safe and that he wouldn't take his medication. She said she was afraid for you kids. When I called my brothers and sisters to tell them I was putting him back in the hospital, they got mad at me, but not a one of them would take him in. Dot, Bernie, even Rip told me I was rotten for not keeping him at home, but not one of them would take him." My father tells me this many years after his father is dead.

The prophetic words of neighbors echo back to me: "There's somethin' funny about them Carpenter kids."

I'm older now, and I want to know the story of Southwood, of going into the hospital, and of going crazy. Did crazy run in my family? I write to request my records. They come in a large manila envelope. When it arrives, there are pages and pages of notes. The jumbled-up, confusing part of my life is all in there: my signature, the intake, the psychiatrist's evaluation, the notes, the medication, my running away, and my release date. It's all written down. I see Like The Fish's signature at the end of his session notes. I didn't make the hospital up. It's real.

Back in the chair, my father blows smoke rings as we look at another photo and article distorted with age.

Fire about 4 a.m. Saturday took the lives of Mrs. Agnes Knapp Car-

penter, 73, and Sharon Sheley, 17, while they were trying to escape from
the burning building. The two-story frame stucco house, which took the
lives of the two women, was located at 815 Union Street. Investigators
theorize the blaze was caused by an overheated stovepipe.

We're having a family reunion and everyone is there—Tim, Dave, Cindi, Mary, Mom, Dad, Uncle Joe, Cousin Cathy. I casually mention the fire and the overheated stovepipe. I bring out the newspaper article and pass it around from relative to relative. "Stovepipe? No, that's not what happened," says Uncle Joe emphatically. "She smoked in bed. Smoked like a chimney. Caught the house on fire that way."

"Cigarettes and the beer, but don't say I said so," says another relative who shall remain anonymous.

"What was Grandma like?" I ask my siblings.

"She smoked a lot and stumbled across the floor."

"She gave me money to go to the candy store on Rees Street."

"She asked me to stay with her a lot. I think she was lonely."

"My mother was an angel," my father always says.

The elderly woman was lying at the foot of the stairs in the center of
the house. The body of the schoolgirl was found on the floor beside her
bed in an upstairs room.

Firemen were prevented for 45 minutes from entering the building
to search for the bodies because the flames were burning out of control.
According to James M. Stage, police patrolman at Clayton and secretary
of the Clayton Volunteer Fire Department, the blaze is believed to have
started from an overheated stovepipe.

Dr. John Fawkes, Clayton, appointed coroner's physician, said the
victims died of suffocation.

At the family reunion, my father and I are sitting alone in my kitchen while everyone else stands around the barbecue outside.

"Tell it to me again," I beg him.

"It was in the middle of the night. I heard the sirens. Then I got a phone call from Mrs. LaLonde. She told me to get over to my mother's house. I ran over to Union Street . . . "

"That's not what happened," my mother yells. She's been hiding in the living room. When she hears the story, she gathers her strength and comes into the kitchen, pushing her walker in front of her. "How would you know? You were always off selling encyclopedias. I'm the one who got the calls from your mother. 'Josephine, come and help me. Ben's trying to bash my brains in with a hammer,' she'd say. I'm the one who had to call the loony bin to take him away. You didn't know." My father's lips go tight.

"My mother was an angel," my father says when my mother leaves the room.

After my mother is gone, a wall falls down in my father's memory, and he tells me the story once again slowly and softly.

Mirror, mirror, on the wall, tell me the truth once and for all.

"It was the middle of the night. I was woken up by the fire sirens. Then the telephone rang, and I went downstairs to answer it. 'Carl,' Mrs. LaLonde said, 'get over to your mother's house right away.' 'Why?' I asked her. 'Just get over there, Carl.' I went upstairs and pulled up my pants and ran as fast as I could up Theresa Street. I could see flames and smoke over by my mother's house. I ran onto Union Street—our house was on fire. The fire engine was pulling water from the hydrant, and firemen were hosing down the roof. Neighbors were huddling together across the street and on the lawn. Charlie Stage was there trying to keep everything under control. The Sheleys were crying out Sharon's name and being held back by the firemen. Your Uncle Rip was standing on the sidewalk, just staring at the house. 'Where's Mom?' I asked him. He didn't say a word, just pointed at the house." My father's face looks cloudy now. His brow is furrowed, and his voice is choked and wobbly. "We lost Mom and Sharon. We lost everything. Nothing else mattered." My father looks away and then back at me. "My mother was an angel."

The burned house is located near the banks of French Creek Bay, which afforded a clean sweep for the wind. The flames were being fanned by a southwest breeze.

Diving and Emerging

I stand, a girl of nine, fat and budding in my two-piece cobalt-blue spandex bathing suit on the dilapidated wooden dock at Mercier's Beach before the mighty St. Lawrence River. The sky is gray and swirling. The river is green and frothy. The waves have little teeth. Pihh, I don't care. My arms lift and my toes point as I do my best Olympic diver imitation. Suddenly, I spring into the air and slice into the water.

It is like a Jell-O parfait in a Tupperware cup. The top layer of water is kiwi colored like old green sea glass. Below it, where there should have been a layer of whipped cream, is a thin layer of light. I swim through the green water and the layer of light down to the middle layer. It is dark-chocolate, brackish water. Below that is another layer of white light. I swim through those layers until, finally, I am in the deepest layer of water parfait near the sandy, sloped bottom. It is clear and warm like the ocean. I scull my arms back and forth like a waiting angel.

I whisk at the sand with my hand but see nothing. My body is still and quiet, barely making a ripple. What am I looking for? I stop, swim, and sweep somewhere else. I repeat this and scatter myself here to there. Swim. Sweep. Stop. Swim. Sweep. Stop. Then—aiee! I find it!

Right there, on the floor of the St. Lawrence River, is a big gold coin left by Blackbeard or some other pirate on his way through the Thousand Islands region of northern New York to kill Napoleon during the Revolutionary War! I snatch the coin. My legs pump through the clear water, the layer of light, the brackish water, and more light. Then, in the green water, I pause and stare up at the sun shining like a portal to the upper world. Clutching the coin, I swim toward the light. The top of the water moves up. I flutter-kick my legs, swimming harder. The top moves up. No matter how hard I swim, the top of the water just keeps moving up. My chest burns and tightens.

I have to take a breath I have to take a breath I have to take a breath I have to take a breath I have to take a breath I have to take a breath my voice repeats inside my head.

Flailing now, I swim desperately. Staring at the sun, I try to get through the portal, but it keeps moving up.

I have to take a breath I have to take a breath I have to take a breath I have to take a breath I have to . . . My mouth opens, and I suck in a big, watery, green breath. *Maawaaahh.*

I sit bolt upright in my yellow-and-orange bedroom that still smells singed from the cotton-ball-extremely-flammable scientific experiment. My sheets are tangled around my feet, and my sweaty nightgown is plastered against my chest. It's dark and quiet in the house, and I can hear my parents snoring. Sitting in the darkness, I feel something in my hand. Something is poking into my palm. *It's the gold coin! I have brought it up from the dream world!* I think. My eyes close in anticipation, and I turn my head away. Slowly uncurling my fingers one at a time, I turn back to see . . . nothing. My hand is empty. It's just my fingernails poking into my palm. I haven't brought the coin up from the dream world. I shove my hands under the blankets, feeling so disappointed. *It isn't fair! I deserve the coin. Hadn't I gone down and made it back up?* I think.

I had that dream for two weeks when I was nine years old and then forgot it. I never thought about the dream again until my second son, Sam, was born. I married Brian, my knight in shining armor, when I was twenty-three years old. We carried on the Carpenter tradition of being poor and resourceful. Curbside chairs and couches adorned our house of treasures. I thought we had a love-never-dies love, but things would change in the coming years. I had a midterm miscarriage before Will was born, sick and mewling. I recognized him as an old friend with a new face. Sam blasted in four years after that at a weight one could only describe as "heifer-like." During Sam's birth, I heard a voice inside my head say *Name him Samuel Joseph.* "His name is Samuel Joseph!" I shouted out. Years later, while poring over birth, burial, and baptismal documents with my cousin Wendy, I discovered that my great-grandfather Carpenter's name was Samuel Joseph.

A caul wearer is believed to have the ability to hear spirits.

Sam is about three weeks old and strapped into his baby carrier in the front seat of my gray Buick. We are rushing home from the grocery store to meet Will at the school bus. Rounding the corner, I glance over at Sam. He is covered with spit-up and milky gurgle.

Oh, he's so perfect, I think.

And suddenly, the dream bubbles up and floods me with its memory.

Anticipation. Struggle. Success. Disappointment.

Why now? Why are you bothering me now when I haven't thought of you in so many years? I ask.

I hold my baby in my arms and greet my son at the bus. We go inside and eat peanut butter and grape jelly sandwiches. In the coming years, I will take Will and Sam to the swimming hole and teach them to swim and dive for treasure in shallow, calm, clear water. They hate me and love me and hate me and love me—the usual. When they cut themselves, I apply the butterfly bandage and give them butterfly kisses in the grass.

It isn't perfect or predictable. Our love rises and falls like the river and the seasons and death and resurrection. Like their mother, they will dive down to look for the gold coin of themselves and emerge into an imperfect world of love and separation and love again. They're Carpenter kids.

Author Interview

The story "The Piano" begins and ends with the words "I'm a Carpenter kid." What does it mean to be a Carpenter kid at the beginning and ending of this story? How has your understanding of yourself and your family changed as you have matured?

Our family was looked down upon as "poor white trash," and the beginning of the story tells you why! We were troublemakers descended from a long line of troublemakers. Feeling like we had to live up to the expectation that we were bad, we certainly didn't disappoint. There was a sense of shame as well, of course, that we were Carpenters. The shadow of our ancestors engulfed us, as it did everyone in our town. We knew and they knew who and where we came from, and that was that. The die was cast. As Carpenter kids, we didn't even have names. We were "Carl's kids." I was so strongly identified with my father, and I identified myself as my father's daughter. It was only in my adulthood that I started thinking about my mother's influence on my life. This story was one of the first that featured my mother.

When writing something, I ask a lot of questions like "Is that true? Were we terrible? What else were we?" I started collecting memories of my mother—little things like butterfly kisses in the grass, her teaching me to spell, making papier-mâché heads at the house on Mary Street, and also the falling out we had when I was sixteen. That estrangement only deepened as time went by. As I compile memories around certain events, I get a broad spectrum of experiences that are contradictory. Life is so full of contradictions. In the middle swirl of all things possible lies what's real, and that's what I'm looking for. "The Piano" started when I asked "Is it possible to hate your mother? Is it possible that she isn't who I am making her out to be?" In a deep way, the story is a shift from being my father's daughter to my mother's daughter. It's also a shift from being an unloved child to a loved child. The story changed into a feeling of pride when I thought of my brothers and sisters giving up their allowance for me and the risk my mother took buying the piano and paying on it for twelve years. At the end of the story, I feel proud to be a Carpenter. I suppose the story is about deciding for myself who we are.

Though all the stories are filled with unforgettable scenes, which ones are the most memorable for you?

I think cinematically and often begin a story with a single image or scene that won't let me go. I build the image stitch by stitch and add other sensory remembrances into it. Tapping into all the senses fleshes out the memory in the reader and allows the reader to tap into his or her set of memories. Some of the strongest images for me are of the St. Lawrence River during the four seasons and the smells and sounds of the river throughout the day. The smells of my parents, too—from my mother's coffee breath to my father's VO5, his cigarettes, his pipe smoke, his aftershave. Even just writing them, I can smell them. It was the river that really captured my memory, however. Clayton is at the mouth of the river and Lake Ontario. The vista is very wide and expansive. When you stand on the docks in

Clayton, you see water and sky. The first time I saw the Mississippi River, it looked like a creek to me! The St. Lawrence River is majestic and bold. There's the cold, the white ice, the sounds of ice cracking apart, the different sounds of snow telling me how cold it was outside. All of these memories click in my head when I think of them. A few of my favorite images, though, are my mother's guitar-shaped body, sidewalks that resemble a seven-year-old's wonky teeth, and my guidance counselor, who was really a barn owl impersonating an alcoholic.

Why do you think the book is titled *Where There's Smoke, There's Dinner?*

Well, this could have been a title for a family cookbook! Family means disaster and danger and chaos, but also routine, normalcy, and everyday experiences. I've always felt that life, love, home, and family are dangerous but comforting. Almost like a teddy bear with a tack in it. Despite the craziness in the house, there was an underlying sense of indestructible love and normalcy. We all got to school most days, went to religious education, had dinner together, and said our prayers at night.

How is the St. Lawrence River like "a mother" to the children in Clayton?

Clayton follows the contours of the St. Lawrence River. It's impossible to go more than ten blocks away from the river. It was a womb that held the town, and in its waters we grew. I lived on the "Frenchie" side of town. This was the Catholic side of town, as opposed to the side of town that was closer to Goose Bay. The Catholics settled on the side of town near French Creek, pronounced "crick," because we were trappers, boat builders, fishermen, guides, and loggers. We worked the river for a livelihood, built a church, and, in the

1700s and 1800s, spoke only French. The Protestants and Baptists near Goose Bay were merchants. There was an invisible line drawn between James and John Streets. I asked my father once why we never went to the Goose Bay side of town, and he replied, "Well, hell, we're Frenchies. We stay on our side of town." Although he had never told me that specifically, I knew it. Riding my bike across town to Goose Bay was like riding over into foreign soil. We rarely did it. They didn't come into our side of town either. It wasn't like there was open animosity between us, just a sense of *ours and theirs*, if you know what I mean. So the river was like a mother to us Catholic kids because it held us in its arms, engulfed us, rocked us, startled us, and taught us lessons about life and death. To me, a mother is both comfort and danger, and the St. Lawrence was that too. It gave us a life and took our lives regularly and without warning or mercy.

Where There's Smoke, There's Dinner **tells the story of a dysfunctional and remarkably original family with humor and compassion. Tell me more about how this was your normal.**

As I told you, we lived on the Frenchie side of town, and everybody from James Street to Reese Street was a Catholic. There was a lot of craziness, and that craziness seemed really normal. It was a hotheaded, passionate side of town. We thought we were normal because we were surrounded by families as crazy as ours. There was a lot of alcoholism and poverty and downright strangeness that just seemed normal.

You state, "In my hometown, you're never who you are, only who you come from." How did being a Carpenter kid limit and liberate you?

It took me a long time to realize if I could never do anything right, I could also never do anything wrong! There was a sense of weight around being a "Carpenter kid" but also a sense of place within my community. I felt like I belonged, in a strange sense, to a family, a community, and a culture. I had something to push against in my hometown: the invisible marks of family and ancestry and small-town small-mindedness. In that sense, I knew who I was to others within a communal context. That allowed me to define who I am to myself.

How did life change when your mother bought the store? How did her resourcefulness provide for the family?

My mother was a quiet and aloof woman with a strong work ethic and a deep devotion to her children. She got into quite a spot when she married my father. He had been wounded in the Second World War physically and psychologically, and he couldn't hold a job because of either his behavior or his hospitalizations. She was up the creek without a paddle. She always made the best of things, though. When she got my Dad's back pay, she bought the store before he could get home and spend it. The store really saved our lives and brought us out of poverty. The store also gave us a place of status in Clayton because people paid all their bills there. My mother knew how much so-and-so was spending on what and to whom. She also sent telegraph messages for people. She was privy to information most people keep private. In that way, she was a bit like a priest who knows what you've done but keeps quiet about it.

How would you describe your parents' relationship to one another? Describe their relationship to the children.

My parents had a fiery, intense, passionate, and complicated love for one another. They were married for over sixty years, and the pendulum swung widely the entire time. My father was a womanizer, unreliable, charming, and charismatic as well as resourceful, openhearted, committed to his family, and a good friend who would give his last dollar to anyone. My mother was quiet, aloof, smart, and hardworking. They had so much misfortune. Some of it they chose, and some of it was thrown on them. Despite their ups and downs, my parents always seemed to fit together. I always felt like my parents had a "true love." During the interviewing for the story "Love is War," Pop said, "The first time I saw your mother, I knew she was the one." She was "the one," but that didn't mean he was faithful to her. Being unfaithful didn't mean he didn't love her—a contradiction. My father went into the same nursing home as my mother to be near her. As my mother aged, she became mentally ill, and my father took care of her. The wide pendulum of care and caring swung again from my mother to my father. Despite their insanity, they were quite devoted to one another.

What are some of the major themes of the book? How can redemption, understanding, and forgiveness be seen in the stories?

This is a good question. I grew up in the late '50s and '60s when the Catholic Church was a very heavy presence in the home and life of Roman Catholics. This isn't news, but the images and teachings of Roman Catholicism are pretty bizarre, violent, and disturbing. That is in me and my worldview. You know, look what they did to the SON OF GOD! For some reason, though, the violence in the Catholic teachings matched the violence in my home, and so the reality of life and God and death and sin all being alive in the home is very real to me. I know how that sounds, but the extremes of life—the urges, the passions, the uncontrollable needs of humans—grabbed me at a young age. I associated all this with the biological and religious fathers. On the other spectrum, the mother was soft, loving, kind, forgiving, and ever present. My mother and the river as mother became a mixture of all things good and mysterious. Things were there but somehow unattainable. I saw so much suffering in my house, especially with my father's surgeries, and for some reason, my internal frame always put it into the religious teachings of redemption, love, and forgiveness. I am not religious nor do I consider myself a Christian, but the mystical and loving aspects of the church became my frame for understanding my experience.

How does the phrase "one man's trash is another man's treasure" exemplify the challenges and creativity of your family life?

My dad could make silk out of a sow's ear. Going to the dump was really fun, and we weren't the only ones who did it in Clayton. My father could find anything and make it work. The televisions were one example of his ingenuity. He also made transistor radio antennas out of wire hangers and pudding from stale bread, and he made warm, just-about-to-turn-old milk palatable by heaping on teaspoons of sugar, raisins, and cinnamon. He also used to make dough Johnnies, which is yeasted raised dough fried in butter. An old hunger trick is to leave the dough in the middle raw. It takes longer to digest, and we slept soundly through the night. He made things fun. The sense of adventure was palpable when we went to the dump. If he held up a less-than-perfect doll, he didn't see the problems but the possibilities. I also just love that he got six televisions. He was a makeshift kind of guy. My mother was a very talented seamstress, knitter, and crocheter and made many of my clothes well into my teens. She once made me a blue crocheted dress that must have weighed forty pounds! My favorite pair of mittens to this day are the skunk ones, complete with tongue and googly eyes, she made me in second grade.

On another level, I am speaking about how one person can seem like trash to the world but be a treasure in someone else's eyes.

The story "Snap!" is the startling turning point of your book. What was it like to write and share that story?

"Snap!" was a difficult story to write and share but a necessary one for me. My brother Tim was killed in a car accident when he was only fifty-five. After his death, I thought, *So many stories I never knew or heard. What story am I not telling?* "Snap!" was it. I carried around so much shame about my experience that I really didn't think I could survive sharing it. Of course, I know that personal stories aren't just for the artist but also for the listener. I pieced together this story in, first, a five-minute performance piece, and then a twenty-minute version, then thirty-five, fifty, and finally an hour-and-ten-minute version of "Snap!"

I could feel the shame being lifted and the healing and understanding beginning. My life was saved, and my family, decades later, was healed. There is no perfect resolution to that situation or the events except to say that there really is nothing good or bad unless I make it so. I believe in love and redemption and forgiveness. I knew my parents to be good people, and so I went looking for their good and their difficulty and found both. "Snap!" let me grow up. A mature mind can rest in the duality of life. I wanted to be free of my childhood pain, and "Snap!" did that for me. I am very grateful to have this story. I feel like it's my gold nugget treasure. I had to scrape off the dirt and debris to find it, though.

Acknowledgments

I am so grateful to Familius Publishing for the chance to publish this collection and for their belief in these stories.

Unlike a regular writer, I'm an old-fashioned gypsy storyteller who speaks rather than writes stories into life. So when I wanted to turn my family stories into a written book, it felt a little like kissing a porcupine. I wanted to do it, but how? The process of turning breath, gesture, pace, voice, and movement into paragraphs, commas, periods, and spacing on a page was made immeasurably easier with the help and support of my publisher, Familius, and my editor, Kelsey Cummings.

Many people ask me: "Do you tell your family these stories before you tell them publicly?" Yes, I do—then they retell them better. I wish all people who share their family stories, especially the painful ones, could have that experience, because stories remind us that our lives and the lives of our families matter.

I want to thank my family—Cindi and Nana, Dave and Maureen, Tim and Joyce, Dan and Eric, and especially my sons, Will and Sam. Angelina, you are the daughter I never gave birth to but still get to tell what to do. I am grateful to my sister Mary for the care she gave my parents at the end of their lives. Finally, I want to thank my irrepressible parents Jo and Carl. You were "the whole ball of wax."

Another debt of gratitude is owed to my colleagues (who quickly became friends): Noa Baum, Lee-Ellen Marvin, Robin Bady, Loren Niemi, Elizabeth Ellis, and Jo Radner. Lizzie Simkin, your beautiful cello music helped give birth to "Snap!" Thank you to Norah Dooley and *massmouth*, where the five-minute version of "Snap!" was first told. Steffani Raff, thank you for introducing me to Familius and for your support and encouragement throughout my writing and editing.

And finally, I want to thank Marjorie, my dearest and oldest friend. Your kindness, grace, and patience remain forever an inspiration.

About the Author

Regi Carpenter is a storyteller, teacher, coach, and performance artist. She tours her shows and workshops nationally and internation-
ally. In order to write this book, Regi gave up her job as a college
professor and walked dogs for two years. Regi has been awarded
the Parents' Choice Gold Award, the J. J. Reneaux Emerging Artist
Award, the Parents' Guide to Children's Media Award, and the Storytelling World Award. She also won the 2012 Boston story slam.
Her stories have been heard on The Moth, NPR, and The Apple
Seed Radio. Her talk "A Hush in the Room" is a featured TedxTalk.
She is currently using storytelling and writing in bereavement and
palliative care.

regicarpenter.com

About Familius

Welcome to a place where parents are celebrated, not compared. Where heart is at the center of our families, and family at the center of our homes. Where boo-boos are still kissed, cake beaters are still licked, and mistakes are still okay. Welcome to a place where books—and family—are beautiful. Familius: a book publisher dedicated to helping families be happy.

Visit Our Website: www.familius.com

Our website is a different kind of place. Get inspired, read articles, discover books, watch videos, connect with our family experts, download books and apps and audiobooks, and along the way, discover how values and happy family life go together.

Join Our Family

There are lots of ways to connect with us! Subscribe to our newsletters at www.familius.com to receive uplifting daily inspiration, essays from our Pater Familius, a free ebook every month, and the first word on special discounts and Familius news.

Become an Expert

Familius authors and other established writers interested in helping families be happy are invited to join our family and contribute on-line content. If you have something important to say on the family, join our expert community by applying at:

www.familius.com/apply-to-become-a-familius-expert

Get Bulk Discounts

If you feel a few friends and family might benefit from what you've read, let us know and we'll be happy to provide you with quantity discounts. Simply email us at orders@familius.com.

Website: www.familius.com

Facebook: www.facebook.com/paterfamilius

Twitter: @familiustalk, @paterfamilius1

Pinterest: www.pinterest.com/familius

The most important work
you ever do will be within the
walls of your own home.

Lightning Source UK Ltd.
Milton Keynes UK
UKOW01f0452190716

278705UK00010B/51/P